THE POLITICS OF VISUAL LANGUAGE

THE POLITICS OF VISUAL LANGUAGE

Deafness, Language Choice,
and Political Socialization

JAMES ROOTS

CARLETON UNIVERSITY PRESS

Copyright © Carleton University Press, 1999

ISBN 0-88629-345-6 (cloth)
ISBN 0-88629-351-0 (paperback)

Printed and bound in Canada

Canadian Cataloguing in Publication Data

Roots, James, date
       The politics of visual language ; deafness, language choice,
and political socialization

Includes bibliographical references.
ISBN 0-88629-345-6 (bnd)
ISBN 0-88629-351-0 (pbk)

       1. Deaf—Means of communication. 2. Deafness—Social
aspects. I. Title.

HV2395.R66 1999   61.4'2   C98-901030-9

Cover art: *Not my Choice*, Elizabeth Morris's rendition of the Deaf
perspective on childhood cochlear implants.
Cover design: Liz Morris Design; photographer, Tom Rosenthal; and
BCumming Design.
Interior: Lynn's Desktop Publishing.

Carleton University Press gratefully acknowledges the support extended to its
publishing program by the Canada Council and the financial assistance of the
Ontario Arts Council. The Press would also like to thank the Department of
Canadian Heritage, Government of Canada, and the Government of Ontario
through the Ministry of Culture, Tourism and Recreation, for their assistance.

CONTENTS

INTRODUCTION

PEOPLE WHO ARE PRELINGUALLY DEAF face a unique linguistic dilemma which has serious political consequences for them.

Their inability to acquire language "normally", that is orally and aurally, means that a conscious choice must be made *for* them as to the language that will be taught to them. The choice is not merely one of selecting among congeneric languages: it is one of selecting among *modes* of language. One of the options is a *sui generis* language: Sign, a strictly visual-gestural language. The alternative is any congeneric language, which is to say a language rooted in an oral-auditory mode. This choice can thus be categorized as a choice between the modes, methods, and philosophies of "manualism" and "oralism".

Although each method/philosophy has its ferocious supporters and the debate between the two appears irreconcilable, they share one crucial feature: the deaf person's approach to either language must necessarily rely heavily upon visual rather than auditory cues.

The oral method has as its objective the apparent integration of the deaf person into the hearing world by means of simulating competence in auditory language via lipreading, speech therapy, and technical aids. The manual method is concerned with giving the deaf child a language within the visual mode deemed most natural (and hence most likely to result in real competence) to him/her; a vital component to the success of this approach is integration into the Deaf Culture.

The choice of method of language acquisition shapes the political socialization of the prelingually deaf child. Regardless of the method chosen, however, the result of the political socialization is a form of marginalization. Exactly what form that marginalization may take is in turn largely determined by the language choice.

TERMINOLOGY

The lower-case *d* "deaf" is a medical label encompassing all individuals in whom the sense of hearing is non-functional for the ordinary purposes of living. The upper-case *D* "Deaf" is a sociological identifier referring only to those deaf people who are recognized and accepted as members of the Deaf Culture (Canadian Association of the Deaf, 1994c). The language of this culture is Sign; thus, it can be assumed that a "Deaf" person and a "manualist" person are synonymous.[1] Oralism is a pathological approach considered by many to be an extension of "the medicalization of deafness" (Stokoe, 1980; Padden and Humphries, 1988; Sacks, 1989; Wilcox, 1989; Lane, 1992); thus, deaf people who are oralists are assigned the "small-*d* deaf" medical label.

It is important for the reader to keep these distinctions in mind, for I will be referring to both "Deaf people" and "deaf people" throughout, and they are *not* interchangeable terms. When speaking of both groups together in a non-medical context, "D/deaf" will be used. The exception is in specific reference to young children, who are always "deaf" because it is assumed they have not yet been enculturated one way or the other. When reference to the medical fact of deafness (regardless of enculturation) is intended, I will use the phrase "people who are deaf" or, secondarily, "deaf people".

Deaf people of both stripes must be distinguished from a third group, the hard of hearing. The latter, as the term implies, are not medically deaf but have suffered some degree of hearing loss. The loss has either occurred after the acquisition of oral-auditory language skills and enculturation into hearing society, or is not of such severity as to seriously handicap the process of language acquisition and enculturation. By definition, therefore, the hard of hearing person wishes to remain as active a participant in hearing society as possible, and to this end utilizes lipreading and technical aids rather than Sign.

Yet another group that should be identified separately is the deafened. These are people who, like the hard of hearing, have grown up more or less hearing and integrated into hearing culture, but who have become severely or profoundly deaf later in life. The lateness of the onset often makes it difficult for them to acquire Sign skills and to integrate fully into the Deaf Culture; they are also different from the oral deaf by virtue of their natural acquisition and long practice of oral-auditory skills. At the same time, their near-complete deafness leaves them an ill fit amongst the hard of hearing, not to mention the hear-

---

[1] The reverse, however, is not true: a "manualist" is anyone, deaf or hearing, who supports Sign. Likewise, an "oralist" is anyone who supports oralism, but an oral deaf person is not necessarily an oralist: he/she may have been raised under the oral system and can still use oral skills but prefers Sign.

ing. Indeed, the deafened are a unique segment deserving of greater study.

The term "hearing impaired", widely adopted by hearing society in the belief that it is polite, is in fact abhorred by Deaf people and has been formally rejected by both the Canadian Association of the Deaf and the Canadian Hard of Hearing Association. The two groups argue that deaf, Deaf, deafened, and hard of hearing people are highly distinctive and cannot be bundled together as a single homogeneous group.

This book focuses upon people who are prelingually deaf, which is to say people who are either born deaf or become deaf before acquiring significant oral-auditory language competence.

SIGN LANGUAGE

The language of the Deaf community, Sign, is properly capitalized in common with any other recognized language such as English and French (World Federation of the Deaf, 1991). In Canada the most common Sign language is American Sign Language (ASL). Canadian francophones use *la Langue des Signes* (or *Sourds*) *du Québec* (LSQ). The differences between these legitimate Sign languages and artificial sign systems (Manually Coded English) are explicated in chapter 2.

Sign is not a written language. Stokoe (1960), Klima and Bellugi (1979), Kyle and Woll (1985), and other researchers have established the grammar, syntax, and semantics of Sign that confirm it as a complete and distinct language which is articulated in space and time.[2] It is not a codification of "English on the hands"; in fact, fingerspelling (the manual alphabet), which hearing people often mistake for "the sign language", is not even considered a formal component of Sign because it is a simple transliteration of the English alphabet (Padden and Humphries, 1988:7).[3]

Stokoe (1960) identified the building blocks of Sign as designators (handshape), tabulators (location of the sign), and signifiers (movement/action of hands). To this list Friedman (1977) and Battison (1978) added orientation (the spatial relation of the hands to each

---

[2] Petitto (1994) has also established Sign as a "real" language on a biological basis.
[3] Fingerspelling does, however, have a role in Sign: it is used to create "loan" signs such as "B-U-S" and "J-O-B".

other and to the body). Baker and Cokely (1980:80) point out that even this list does not cover the full spectrum of Sign: there are some signs, often called "affective markers", which are totally non-manual, such as a twitching of the nose which communicates the colloquial message, "Yeah, I know" or "Yeah, I agree".

The nature of these building blocks suggests why it is unlikely that a facile and widely adopted written form of Sign can be developed. Stokoe and others developed a written notation of the grammar, but a notation is all it is or attempts to be. Valerie Sutton invented "Sutton Movement Writing"; this is no more a practical *everyday* written language than is Stokoe's notation. Attempting to create a written Sign language is wryly described by Stokoe as an "effort to transcribe in two dimensions a language whose syntax uses the three dimensions of space as well as time" (Sacks, 1989:78n).

Sacks, who is sympathetic to Deaf Culture, nonetheless muses that if a written form of Sign were to be adopted by the Deaf, "it might lead them to a written literature of their own, and serve to deepen their sense of community and culture" (1989:79n). But in historical fact the lack of a written literature has been a significant contributor to Deaf people's already intense sense of community and culture: Deaf people need to see each other in person to communicate, gossip, exchange information, and simply to socialize without the linguistic tensions they experience every day in their interactions with the hearing world.

Suggestions that the unwritten nature of Sign might be a factor in the high rate of functional illiteracy among the Deaf are misplaced. Facility in one written language (English, for example) is not a guarantor of facility in a second language (Spanish or French, or ASL for that matter). Studies have proven that early first-language competence can predict success in second-language acquisition: this applies to the Deaf children of Deaf parents who acquire ASL first and later score better on English literacy tests than deaf children of hearing parents who fail to acquire early competence in either ASL or English (Carver, 1988a).

What Sign language *does* entail for most Deaf people is that they must become bilingual in Sign and in the dominant language of their society. More than that, they must become *bimodally* competent: in visual-gestural language, and in oral/aural-written language. It is bimodalism which proves the real challenge to their ability to function in the dominant society, because to a great extent it determines their ability to communicate with and within that society. In turn, their ability to communicate with and within the dominant society is a powerful influence upon their ability and their desire to integrate into it.

DEMOGRAPHICS

The 1986-87 Health and Activities Limitations Survey (HALS, "the disability census") reported that four of every hundred Canadians (1,022,220) "have impaired hearing which may present barriers to their daily activities" (Schein, 1992:1). A total of 3.5 percent (i.e., 30,130) use Sign language either alone or in combination with lipreading (*ibid.*, 19). About 10.4 percent (nearly 3,700) attend "a special school", 34.4 percent (12,229) attend mainstreamed classes, and 43.5 percent (15,464) are integrated in regular schools.

For nearly a decade, I have been a consultant and critic in the preparation and analysis of both the Canada Census and the Health and Activities Limitations Survey. Nonetheless, it is my contention (supported by Padden and Humphries, 1988:4-5) that not a single accurate or reliable statistic on Deaf Canadians exists.

HALS's definition ("have impaired hearing which may present barriers to ... daily activities" [Schein, 1992:1]) may have resulted in an unknown number of culturally Deaf people excusing themselves from the census on the grounds that, since their daily lives revolve around Deaf friends and Deaf socializing, they experience no barriers to such activities. Furthermore, the sub-division of respondents into three categories arranged by self-reported ability to hear in individual or group conversations is not only unreliable but blurs the distinction between hard of hearing, Deaf, deaf, and deafened persons.

HALS similarly fails to isolate Deaf users of Sign language as a first language or equivalent-to-first language. Its distinction between the use of Sign alone or in combination with lipreading is a false one because lipreading cannot be isolated from the reading of facial expression which is an integral part of Sign. And its figures on schooling are obsolete because the push for the educational integration of disabled students occurred well after the 1986 HALS.

The Canadian Association of the Deaf adheres to the formula of applying U.S. demographics to the Canadian population. According to this method, one in ten Canadians (2.6 million) has a hearing loss of some degree; one in 100 (260,000) is profoundly deaf; and one in 1,000 (26,000) uses Sign as a first language. The Canadian Hard of Hearing Association agrees with this formula and uses it to calculate that 2.5 million Canadians are hard of hearing; unfortunately, this number includes an unknown percentage of oral deaf people, which further clouds the statistical picture. In any case, the very basis of this formula too is suspect, since as a rule American statistics rarely extrapolate fittingly into Canadian circumstances.

ACKNOWLEDGEMENTS

The author would like to thank the National Literacy Secretariat for its financial assistance toward the publication of this book. I would also like to thank Professor Sharon Sutherland for her tireless scrutiny of this study; Professor Bob Jackson for his encouragement and support; and Roger Carver for going beyond the role of mere reviewer to play the devil's advocate as well.

Special thanks, of course, to my wife Dot and children Emerson, Genevieve, and Monika, for their love, support, patience, and tolerance through the research and rewriting of this book.

I

POLITICAL SOCIALIZATION
AND MARGINALIZATION

SOCIALIZATION

SOCIALIZATION IS THE PROCESS of learning socially relevant behaviours in order that the individual may function within a given society or social group (Adler and Harrington, 1970:2). It involves not only learning but internalizing group patterns, values, and feelings so that the individual "not only knows what is expected of him and behaves accordingly; he also feels that this is the proper way for him to think and behave" (Elkin, 1960:4).

Descriptions of socialization assume three pre-existing conditions. One is that the society into which the individual is being socialized does in fact exist and possesses values, patterns, culture, norms, status, roles, and standards of right and wrong and of appropriate behaviour, all of which have been developed historically before the child is born (Elkin, 1960). While this may seem a tautological requirement, it points up the significance of the implication that the society's characteristics have been *institutionalized*. There must be well-defined structures and organizations to act as socializing influences and training grounds. For example, the behaviours and roles inculcated by the school can subsequently be generalized to other social arenae, including the political life of the community (Hess and Torney, 1967).

The second condition for socialization is variously defined as "human nature" (Elkin, 1960:7), "the ability to establish emotional relationships with others" (*ibid.*), and "social contexts" such as class, ethnicity, and regionalism (Hess and Torney, 1967). The second condition might thus be generally described as personal and group interrelationships, ranging from family and friends to school classmates, organization memberships, religious congregations, and larger groups identified by sexual preferences, socio-economic status, racial or linguistic distinctions, geographical location, or other marks.

The third condition for socialization is the individual him/herself and his/her characteristics and capabilities. Elkin calls this condition the individual's "biological inheritance" and explains that if a particular individual is lacking in this regard, for example through "feeble-mindedness", then "adequate socialization becomes extremely difficult, if not impossible" (1960:7). Adler and Harrington explicate that "socialization is not a simple transfer of behaviour from one generation to another": the process involves teaching and learning "cognitive maps that enable the individual to sort out and make sense of the diversity of social roles and persons which make up his environment" (1970:4). If there is a "biological" obstacle within the individual which interferes with his/her ability to perform his/her part of the process, the result may be isolation, deprivation, alienation, or psychopathology.

The deaf child's "biological inheritance" is the single most important element influencing his/her socialization. The deafness does not itself shape his/her socialization; rather, it is the given against which society reacts in ways that will determine the child's enculturation, his/her personal and group interrelationships, and his/her receptivity to the socializing content. These societal reactions are more than usually variable, unpredictable, and traumatizing (for both the subject and the agencies) because they are always rooted in the society's identification of, and its attempts to deal with, the deafness as a perceived instrument of interference with the normal *media* of socialization.

POLITICAL SOCIALIZATION

Adler and Harrington build upon the classic definition of socialization for their definition of political socialization, arguing that the latter consists of "the process whereby children are socialized to the norms and values of society that have to do with political events, institutions, and ideas" (1970:1).

Greenstein broadly defines political socialization as "all political learning, formal and informal, deliberate and unplanned" (1965:551). Dawson (1977:60, 78-79, ch. 6) criticizes this definition on the grounds that political learning and political socialization are not synonymous but complementary. Dawson's own attempts at a definition, however, seem more succinct than satisfactory: he has described political socialization variously as "the developmental process through which the citizen matures politically" (1969:17) and as "the personal and social origins of political outlooks" (1977:1). The former definition echoes an earlier proposal by Easton and Dennis (1969:7), who see political socialization as "those developmental processes through which persons acquire political orientations and patterns of behaviour."

Perhaps the most satisfactory definition is Sigel's (1970:xii):

Political socialization refers to the process by which people learn to adopt the norms, values, attitudes, and behaviors accepted and practiced by the ongoing system. Such learning, however, involves much more than the acquisition of the appropriate knowledge of a society's political norms and more than the blind performance of appropriate political acts; it also assumes that the individual so makes these norms and behaviors his own — internalizes them — that to him they appear to be right, just, and moral.

THEORETICAL FRAMEWORKS OF POLITICAL SOCIALIZATION

Herbert Hyman

By drawing together numerous studies on the political and social development of young people and analyzing them in his book *Political Socialization* (1959), Hyman laid the foundations of political socialization as a distinct field. His conclusions, as may be expected of a pioneer study, were broad and tentative.

Essentially, Hyman saw political socialization as the development of the individual's political outlook, a process shaped principally by the family, the school, and the peer group. The child is father to the man: *"humans must learn their political behavior early and well and persist in it"* (Hyman, 1959:10; italics in original). Where the child is able to feel he/she has some degree of political power in his/her immediate relationships, and where the family demonstrates an interest in political events and activity, he/she is more likely to grow up with political interests and to feel politically efficacious.

While Hyman was hesitant to draw conclusions, he affirmed that the primary political socialization goal of the *society* was to ensure its own perpetuation. Since Hyman's chief interest lay in the development of the individual's political outlook, he did not pursue this point.

Fred Greenstein

Greenstein conducted surveys of New Haven children between 1958 and 1964 which focused upon the political learning of the pre-adult years. These surveys appeared to substantiate Hyman's hypothesis that the first thirteen years of life are the most influential years as far as political socialization is concerned; since these years are spent largely within the family structure, the family is logically the single most powerful agent of socialization.

Greenstein suggested the importance of early learning lies in the fact that it occurs during a formative period "of great plasticity and receptivity" (1965:79). The immature child learns uncritically, nonconsciously, and at a time when his/her fundamental personality characteristics are being formed. Early learning determines "which segments of reality are selected and incorporated into the individual's frame of reference" (81). Quoting Harvey and associates (*Conceptual Systems and Personality Organization*, 1961), Greenstein went on to explain that this frame serves as "an experiential filter through which impinging events are screened, gauged, and evaluated, a process which determines in large part what responses can and will occur" (81-82).

Naturally, the familial situation has a strong effect upon the development of the child's frame of reference. Greenstein found that "the importance of political roles clearly is learned quite early, before the age of nine" (1965:32). Since the actual roles themselves are fairly vague to young children, the recognition of their importance must be rooted in feelings and opinions which are communicated to the child by his/her own familiar authorities, i.e., the parents. "Political information increases substantially over the brief age span [between nine and fourteen] ... but the structure of factual knowledge is erected on a foundation of feelings, assessments, and opinions" (35). By adolescence, "a large proportion of the political orientations which guide the participation of adult voters are already present" (44).

Borrowing from psychoanalytic theory, Greenstein further speculated that children make the transition from family to society by transferring the political lessons of the family structure to the society's political system. For an American child, as an example, the political authority of the father is found to be analogous to the authority of political leaders such as the President. Such a development confirms, for Greenstein, the long-held psychological and anthropological argument that whatever is learned earliest in life has "great influence on lasting personality characteristics"; moreover, it is these elements which prove most resistant to change (53).

A major exception to this rule is Greenstein's finding that political *issues* tend to remain poorly understood and difficult to judge even when the child is clear and decisive concerning political party orienta-tions. According to Greenstein, this may be due to two factors: one, young children have not yet developed the ability to think in the abstract terms required to grasp complex issues; and two, family polit-ical orientations are learned very early (albeit unconsciously) as a part of the child's development of a self-identification. This latter point will become significant later in this paper when I discuss the politics of the family of a deaf child; the former point anticipates the work of Petitto, Bellugi, and others on how visual/gestural language is needed as a tool in the building of a deaf infant's cognitive map.

David Easton

Easton built upon Hyman's note that the primary driving force of political socialization, both as a process and as an end, is the state's objective of cultivating support for itself. Working with a variety of col-laborators over the years, Easton applied a systems analysis approach to political socialization that viewed the latter as a process which aimed not only to teach political outlooks but to aggregate them in ways that have consequences for the political life of the nation (Dawson, Prewitt, and Dawson, 1977:14).

Easton and Dennis (1969) observed that the basic political princi-ples of the American state, such as federalism and majoritarianism, have remained essentially intact over the two hundred years of the existence of the United States. Such persistence cannot be taken for granted: stresses do exist upon the system, both externally and internally. For example, one function of the state is to reward and punish, and this may occur in ways that may imperil loyalty to the system: economic injustice, discrimination on racial or sexual bases, and even progressive income taxation tend to reward some individuals at the expense of others. How does the state manage the resultant unhappiness and inequality?

Easton and Dennis suggested that the state must socialize its mem-bers to grant it "diffuse support", an unconditional trust and confi-dence which is strong enough to sustain one's support of the system even as one is being "punished" by its decisions: "My country, right or wrong." This inclination of the individual to continue to provide dif-fuse support is not natural: it must be developed by means of political socialization. Thus, political socialization is clearly focused upon the good of the system rather than the individual.

Easton and Dennis traced the internalization of diffuse support principally to the schools (in contrast to Hyman and to Greenstein, who identified the family as the key socializing agency, but in agreement with Hess and Torney, who were quite firm in bestowing that honour upon the school). They argued that schools perform four socializing functions, as follows:

1. *Politicization.* The school acts as the agent which pries the child out of "the exclusive bonds of the family and make[s] it possible for him to reach out to the structure of political authority" (1969: 391).

2. *Personalization.* Through the teachings of the school curriculum, political authority takes on concrete form, for example as the President.

3. *Idealization.* The political authority is presented in an idealized way to the child, thus encouraging him to view it in a positive and trusting manner.

4. *Institutionalization.* The child's positive view of political authorities is institutionalized, that is, extended from the individual political leader (personification) to the political institutions of government such as the Senate. The child's idealization is transformed into diffuse support.

A key observation Easton and Dennis made to buttress their theory is that the above four functions performed by the school ensure that "the initial bond between citizen and authoritative institutions is strongly positive" (Dawson, Prewitt, and Dawson, 1977:23); thus, when the child matures and is able to judge critically the actual performance of the political institutions and leaders (or to decide he/she is personally receiving more "punishments" than "rewards" from the state), the strength of the positive initial bond cushions his/her negative feelings.

Richard Dawson

One of the most thorough and detailed theoretical structures of political socialization is that of Dawson (1977). He examined the work of his predecessors and found virtually all of them agreed that early learning is the key to political socialization; however, Dawson argued, their own evidence does not support this belief. Long-term studies indicated that in fact the political outlook and orientations of the mature adult bore little resemblance to those of the pre-adult. Dawson suggested that far from embedding fixed political orientations into the individual, early learning teaches the child political and social identities — "the 'social category system' of his or her particular society" (44) — which "might constitute the core orientations upon which *subsequent* political orientations are built" (45; emphasis added).

Political learning develops in conjunction with the learning of social identities such as class, race, and religion; moreover, all such learning necessarily proceeds only in tandem with the maturing of the functions of the brain itself. "The development of political thinking follows the capacity of the individual to handle abstractions and engage in the types of thinking necessary for understanding social and political relationships" (60). Greenstein and Easton are correct in noting the young child's positive feelings toward political authority, but they overlook the increasing influence of the child's "social category" upon his/her political opinions as he/she matures; "By late childhood or early adolescence ... particular outlooks reflect the picture of the political world one has from one's position as a young black, a young Chicano, or a middle-class white" (62).

Dawson developed two models of political learning: indirect and direct. Indirect learning is a two-step process in which a non-political, almost generic orientation is developed and later applied to political objects; as an example, the child forms relations with parents and teachers which develop his/her framework for dealing with authority, including political authorities as he/she later becomes aware of them. Direct political socialization "refers to processes in which the content of orientations transmitted is specifically political" (96); for example, explicit school lessons about the structure of the government. "The critical distinction between indirect and direct modes of learning is not the overt intent of the socialization agent, but whether or not the initial socialization experience is infused with specific political content" (96).

Dawson recognizes a special importance for marginalized groups in indirect political socialization (although he does not use the term "marginalized"). Their social values may be embedded in their subcultural background; thus, when the time comes in their maturation process to extend their values to external specifically political objects, what results is not a successful integration into the existing system and its values but rather a tension or response divergent from the norms of the dominant society. This may explain the fact that inner-city Black children, for instance, show little trust in political leaders and low feelings of political efficacy. A similar situation may exist for deaf persons, particularly those who come from the Deaf subculture.

Dawson's model of direct political socialization involves four forms of learning: imitation, anticipatory socialization, political education, and political experiences. These forms will be defined and applied to D/deaf students in chapter 3 of this book.

MARGINALIZATION

What happens when the political socialization of an individual may be said to be, for whatever reason, unsuccessful? Elkin (1960) suggested that a failure to socialize may result in isolation, deprivation, or psychopathology. In the field of political socialization, several researchers have identified alienation as the consequence (Seeman, 1959; Marcuse, 1964; Etzioni, 1968). Political philosophers have variously termed the result "displacement" (Elshtain, 1993), "exclusion" (Kymlicka, 1992) "anomie" (Yinger, 1973), and "estrangement" (Friedenberg, 1971). Generally speaking, all these terms might be regarded as elements of the broad concept of "marginalization".

Marginalized persons or groups are those who may be described as being outside the mainstream of society. Young, who considers marginalization "perhaps the most dangerous form of oppression", defines it as "a whole category of people [who are] expelled from useful participation in social life" (1990:53). Their status may have arisen as a social-political reaction to their race, religion, gender, economic status, or what Goffman (1963) labelled "stigma" (such as disability, sexual preference, *demi-monde* occupation, or simply "difference"). Although these people probably share the same civil and political rights as non-marginalized persons, their political socialization may be said to have failed in that the state does not solicit their support and involvement, and/or that they choose or feel compelled not to give their support to the state, and/or that they have not been reconciled to the ongoing political-social system. They are either excluded from it by overt or covert discrimination or they reject it because they are unable to identify with it or do not feel a part of it (Patterson, 1963).

Gergen and Ullman suggest that earlier (pre-adolescent) socialization may render the individual vulnerable to the negative impact of "contemporary structural characteristics" (1977:421). Several studies confirm the early socialization into political inferiority of groups such as Chicanos, Blacks, and women. LaMare (1974) found that Chicanos, for example, express more alienation, powerlessness, and indifference to the system than Anglophones even in their pre-teen years. Liebschutz and Niemi (1974) discovered that by Grade 5, Black children already consider themselves less politically efficacious than other ethnic groups and they view the political system as being less responsive to them; Button (1974) confirmed these findings and extended them to include Anglophone females.

The characteristics of alienation as mapped by Seeman (1975) provide an apt description of marginalization.[1] Seeman identifies *discrepancy* as the key notion of alienation; although there is a variety of opinions as to exactly where the discrepancy is located within social-political power relationships, the core element shared by all opinions is that of a gap between potential and actual mastery (93).

This gap can be found within each of the six varieties of alienation that Seeman identifies: powerlessness (lack of control), meaninglessness (lack of understanding of personal and social affairs), normlessness (deviation from convention), cultural estrangement (rejection of commonly held values), self-estrangement (involvement in unrewarding activities), and social isolation ("the sense of exclusion or rejection vs [*sic*] social acceptance") (93-94). It may be inferred that each of these characteristics indicates some degree of failure of the political socialization process.

Goffman (1963) developed the deviance theory through his analysis of individuals who were marginalized from society because of a "discrediting" difference which he labelled a "stigma". The most obvious examples of such a stigma are physical and mental disabilities, including deafness. Goffman showed that, by definition, the stigmatized person is classified by general society as being "not quite human. On this assumption we exercise varieties of discrimination, through which we effectively, if often unthinkingly, reduce his life chances" (5).[2]

Moreover, the stigmatized person is socialized to internalize this assumption: he/she may come to *agree* that he/she is inferior or a failure and therefore deserving of marginalized status. He/she "acquires iden-

[1]   Caution must be taken not to use the terms "marginalization" and "alienation" interchangably: though closely related (indeed, the latter is often an element of the former), they are not synonymous. The membership of the Reform Party, as an example, consists largely of white, middle-aged or older, financially comfortable, Anglo-Saxon Protestant males — not only not a marginalized group but in fact the very cultural segment alleged to be dominant — yet they joined Reform because they felt alienated from the prevailing political power structures and institutions (Sigurdson, 1994).

[2]   Goffman also suggested that the stigmatization extends to the immediate family members, which may further pressure them to do everything possible to "normalize" the disabled member and thereby regain their own "proper" (non-stigmatized) societal status.

tity standards which he applies to himself in spite of failing to conform to them"; inevitably, the result is self-estrangement and ambivalence as to his/her own identity (106). His/her deviance from the expectations of society excludes the stigmatized person not only from true integration into that society but also potentially from true integration with him/herself. This hypothesis will be seen to be significant in understanding the "identity crisis" of people who are deaf in a hearing society.

Goffman and others (Davis, 1961; Krause, 1965; Sussman, 1972) have emphasized that "difference" in itself is not marginalizing: it is the interaction of the individual with the society that results in marginalization on the basis of the *societal reaction to* the individual's difference: the individual "deviates" from society's expectations and accepted norms. Ironically, the application of deviance theory to disabled persons has come under attack for bolstering that which it criticizes: labelling the disabled as "deviants" actually reinforces the already-extant and handicapping view of someone who is disabled as "negatively valued by, and socially isolated from, the rest of society" (Schwartz, 1988). Bogdan and Taylor (1987), among others, argue instead for a "sociology of acceptance". Such a sociology requires shifting focus away from the interrelationships between disabled and non-disabled persons and toward the disabling versus the enabling environment; in other words, shifting focus away from the personal and toward the socio-political. The socio-political approach advocates anti-discriminatory legislation and laws as the tools by which to take down the marginalizing barriers, on the rationale that "the functional demands exerted on human beings by the environment are fundamentally determined by public policy" (Hahn, 1988:118). This approach is in fact the root of "the politics of identity" (social and political advocacy based upon one's group grievances) which has resulted in concerns about justice, equality, and difference. We shall now examine some of these concerns as expressed by various political and social philosophers.

THEORIES OF POLITICAL MARGINALIZATION

T.H. Marshall

T.H. Marshall, particularly in his famous 1949 essay "Citizenship and Social Class", explored the historical extension of citizenship rights as the state's attempt to minimize political marginalization — to ensure that every person knows him/herself to be a full and equal member of society and the body politic. "We can go on to say that the claim of all to enjoy [the 'standard of civilized life'] is a claim to be admitted to a share in the social heritage, which in turn means a claim to be accepted as full members of the society, that is, as citizens" (76).

Marshall's essay traced the historical development of three dimensions of citizenship. Civil rights, in the form of equal protection under the law, comprised the dominant interpretation of citizenship in the eighteenth century; political rights, in the form of enfranchisement and eligibility for public office (as examples), became recognized in the nineteenth century; social rights, in the form of education, health care, and other basic needs, rose to prominence in the twentieth century (78-81).

Simultaneous with the expansion of the concept of citizenship was the extension of its rights to hitherto excluded segments of the populace: women, religious minorities, racial minorities, and the economic underclasses. "The normal method of establishing social rights is by the exercise of political power, for social rights imply an absolute right to a certain standard of civilization which is conditional only on the discharge of the general duties of citizenship" (103). Broadly speaking, these newly enfranchised segments of a populace are those segments which require the assistance of a liberal welfare state in order to meet their basic needs as well as to carry out their citizenship rights and responsibilities. The state has responded to these needs through such measures as public health care systems, social security programs, and anti-discrimination laws (such as the Canadian Charter of Rights and Freedoms and the U.S. Civil Rights Act).

The diminution of inequality strengthened the demand for its abolition.... Class-abatement is still the aim of social rights, but it has acquired a new meaning. It is no longer merely an attempt to abate the obvious nuisance of destitution in the lowest ranks of society. It has assumed the guise of action modifying the whole pattern of social inequality. (106)

Marshall was led to the conclusion that it was only in a liberal democratic welfare state that every member of the society could feel him/herself to be a full and equal participant. At any point of violation of the three dimensions of citizenship rights, individuals or segments of the populace will be marginalized in that they will either be actually unable to participate fully and equally, or will be viewed by others (rightly or wrongly) as less than full and equal members of the society.

The extension of citizenship rights in most liberal democratic welfare states has achieved much in the way of removing the technical obstacles that conduce toward marginalization. The key word here is *technical*. Since the publication of Marshall's essay, there has been an increase in awareness of *non-technical* means of marginalization, such as systemic discrimination, inadequate or negligent implementation of rights, negative socialization, stigmatization, and the denial of "recognition".

The growth of awareness of these non-technical means of marginalization has exposed a major weakness in Marshall's theory: his focus on the expansionary nature of citizenship rights assumes an overarching common culture into which the various disadvantaged segments of society could, would, and should be folded (Marshall and Bottomore, 1992). To the contrary, the persistence of other-culture adherence and resistance to the "melting-pot" imperative has presented great challenges toward the integration of the marginalized (Bissoondath, 1993). This is most obviously true of those who are "different" from the "common culture" by virtue of their race, foreign heritage, or religion, but it is equally applicable to those who are "different" because of stigma such as sexual preference and in at least one case — that of the Deaf — their disability (Lane, 1986).

Jean Bethke Elshtain

The civil rights movements of the 1960s, coupled with the fresh public sensitivity to social inequality and its manifestations such as systemic discrimination, fueled the growth of "identity politics" in the last quarter of the twentieth century. The attributes — the stigmata, in Goffman's terminology — which have been used to marginalize an individual are now often transformed into the political identity through which that person not only demands his/her "rights" but through which he/she also proclaims both personal authenticity and political credibility (57). Elshtain (1993:52) calls this situation "a politicized ontology":

Persons are more and more judged not by what they do or say but by what they *are*. What you are is what your racial or sexual identity dictates. One's identity becomes the sole and only ground of politics, the sole and only determinant of political good and evil. Those who disagree with my "politics", then, are the enemies of my identity.

Identity politics inevitably lead to re-tribalization, as allegiance to "the common culture" breaks down in favour of allegiance to the members of one's stigma-group: "The citizen gives way before the aggrieved member of a self-defined group" (52). The great danger is that this shift of allegiance sets up a "politics of displacement", that is to say, a politics in which the *celebration* of marginalization (rather than its deplorableness) becomes the focus (57). Elshtain fears that this situation endangers democracy itself, for communication and commonality both vanish: "Difference more and more becomes exclusivist.... There [becomes] no way that we can negotiate the space between our pregiven differences" (75).

Elshtain's analysis is particularly relevant to people who are deaf, given that they have always been marginalized on the basis of their stigma (Lane, 1986). Their social and political status has been improved somewhat only recently, precisely *because* they finally evolved a "political ontology" based on their identity as culturally Deaf people. Elshtain raises interesting questions as to the extent to which this pathway can continue to be profitably pursued by the Deaf.

Charles Taylor

Taylor shares many of Elshtain's concerns about "identity politics". He begins his analysis with a critique of the Goffmanesque perspective on self-identity, which he believes fuels the sort of "political ontology" described by Elshtain. To argue that marginalization can arise from society's failure to reflect the full spectrum of its own human makeup, rather than merely its White Anglo-Saxon Christian male segment, is to argue that one's identity is shaped by its reflection (or absence of reflection) in the mirror of the media. Taylor believes that instead our identity is inwardly generated through an active dialogical process with others; thus the crucial importance of recognition by others — *recognition*, not *reflection* (25, 32, 34).

Recognition involves the extension of acceptance, respect, and dignity of one's difference: it is a politics of difference (not displacement) based on identity. Simultaneous with the development of this form of politics has been the development of "the politics of universalism, emphasizing the equal dignity of all citizens, and the content of this politics has been the equalization of rights and entitlements" (37). Unfortunately, these two varieties of politics contradict each other: the politics of universalism assumes that all are equal and standard, whereas the politics of difference insists upon the recognition and even the fostering of particularity.

Taylor shares Hegel's belief that all humans have a "universal human potential" that entitles them to an acknowledgement of their equal value as human beings. The demand for equal recognition extends beyond this concession to a demand for acknowledgement of what they have made of this potential. How to measure this degree of accomplishment? A universal standard would be not only homogeneous and hence a violation of the politics of difference, it would also inevitably reflect the principles and culture of the dominant group and thus would be discriminatory and marginalizing for the members of other groups.

The argument that difference groupings should be judged only by their own cultural value systems is disturbing to Taylor because it gives rise to relativism: the view that since oppressed cultures are equally valid, they must therefore also be of equal value. Moreover, this kind of judgment would be homogenizing because it would be based on the judges' own standards; that is, "we" would be incorporating the other cultures' values into "our" own canon of values. "By implicitly invoking our standards to judge all civilizations and cultures, the politics of difference can end up making everyone the same" (71).

Taylor does not appear to have a solution to the dilemma, admitting that in fact it is probably insoluble; his conclusion is a call for the Hegelian "presumption of equal worth" in spite of its hopelessly self-contradictory nature.

Iris Marion Young and the Case of Canada

Iris Marion Young's philosophy of cultural pluralism is significant as an attempt to construct a political apparatus that would use explicit recognition and support of cultural difference as a means toward accommodating marginalized segments. In other words, she endeavours to resolve exactly those "insoluble" problems which Taylor identified as being inherent within the politics of difference. She does so by taking the "identity" and "respect" of differences as the given structure to which the political and social community must be adapted, rather than vice versa.

Interestingly, while she explicitly rejects the traditional concession toward a "common" homogeneous culture to which all segments should be assimilated, she also rejects the opposite extreme of an atomized culture in which each member is regarded as an unaffiliated individual and in which individual rights supersede group rights. Young is adamant that political systems must be based on specifically *group* differences, and no group is more equal than another.

Her reasoning is that contemporary Western societies have always privileged some groups above others, and these privileged groups have succeeded in establishing their particular cultural beliefs and objectives as the "common culture" of the society. To insist that the members of other segments should abandon their own cultural identities and assimilate into the overarching "common" one is oppressive and reinforces their marginalization.

The solution to marginalization, Young believes, is twofold. First, the state must provide formal recognition of the marginalized groups (by funding their organizations, for example) and ensure they are represented in the decision-making process (through guaranteed positions in the legislature); and second, the state must respond to their particular needs at the policy level through such means as minority language rights, employment equity, multicultural education, and so on.

Although Young (an American) never mentions Canada, her solutions almost perfectly mirror Canadian social policy at least since the 1971 Multiculturalism Act. Organizations representing marginalized groups, from women to Natives to visible minorities to disabled people, have received funding support from federal and provincial governments. Their demands for guaranteed representation are often accommodated in specific instances, such as the gender balance within the federal Liberal and New Democratic parties, the inclusion of Native representatives in Constitutional discussions, and the establishment of the Court Challenge Fund to guarantee financial support for equality court cases. At the policy level, the Canadian Government has responded through the Multiculturalism Act, the Official Languages Act, the Charter of Rights and Freedoms, and the Employment Equity Act, to cite four prominent instances (Cairns, 1992).

Despite these efforts, it is highly questionable whether Canada's marginalized groups feel they have been allocated their fair share of respect, recognition, influence, and power. The Meech Lake Accord controversy, the *Citizens' Forum on Canada's Future*, and the Charlottetown Accord referendum are only three recent opportunities through which these groups have vented the anger and frustration typical of a marginalized status (Spicer, 1991; McRoberts and Monahan, 1993). Even those political analysts (Alan Cairns, Rainer Knopf,

F.L. Morton, Reg Whitaker) who have raised deep concerns about the power that the groups have gained under the Charter of Rights have concluded that they have actually had their marginalized status *reinforced* rather than broken down (Cairns, 1991; Whitaker, 1992).

Kymlicka (1992) has raised a further concern about Young's philosophy, which he associates with "differentiated citizenship", i.e., allegiance to a group identity instead of, or in addition to, allegiance to the "common" national identity:

Of course, there is no guarantee that group and national identities will be mutually reinforcing. There are also many examples of countries where the institutionalization of group identities and rights has torn the country apart (eg. Lebanon). What then is the source of unity in a society that recognizes differentiated citizenship? (32)

Kymlicka's question is an important one for the consideration of marginalization, because its answer (assuming there can be a satisfactory one) could provide an entrance point through which marginalized groups may overcome their disadvantaged status.

NEGLECT OF THE DISABLED

Researchers in political marginalization have generally demonstrated far less interest in persons with disabilities than in the more "conventional" marginalized groups such as Blacks, women, and gays; disabled people tend to end up as "bit players" in their studies, if they earn mention at all. Young, for example, who at least does refer to people with disabilities, simply tags them onto the end of her various lists of marginalized groups[3] and devotes nearly all her attention to the other members of those lists.

This neglect of the disabled — we might even refer to it as the scholarly "marginalization of the disabled from the ranks of the marginalized" — is bemusing given the basic, intriguing, and terribly important differences between the disabled and those who are marginalized for other reasons. Consider, for example, a superficial comparison of their respective experiences with the four agencies usually cited

---

[3] For example: "women, Blacks, Chicanos, Puerto Ricans and other Spanish-speaking Americans, American Indians, Jews, lesbians, gay men, Arabs, Asians, old people, working-class people, and the physically and mentally disabled" (Young, 1990:40).

as the most significant socializing influences: the family, the schools, the peer group, and the media:

1. *Family.* Those who are marginalized for their race, religion, or gender are born into families whose members share these attributes. Disabled people are nearly all born into families whose other members do *not* share their marginalizing attribute.

2. *Schools.* Most Blacks, Jews, women, and gays (as examples) attend the same schools as anyone else, whether public or private; even those schools segregated by gender are "normal" as far as the school's political socializing function is concerned. Disabled people have historically been sent to "institutions for the handicapped", "experimental schools for the deaf", "model schools for the deaf-blind" — schools which, by definition, are segregated from "normal" society strictly on the basis of a negative stigma and which are often unproductive in the sense of offering limited educational value and encouragement (as shall be seen with respect to the education of the deaf).

3. *Peers.* The movement to integrate disabled students into "normal" schools creates a paradoxical situation *vis-à-vis* that student's peer group. The "institutions for the handicapped" and the schools for the deaf, deaf-blind, and blind at least had the advantage of surrounding the disabled child with others who shared his/her stigma; within the context of a normal school, that child is usually surrounded by non-stigmatized peers. These circumstances may be similar for students who belong to a religious or racial minority (i.e., a student may be the only Asian in his class) but the latter may still function as a "normal" within the peer group; placing a disabled student inside a non-disabled peer group creates a further *disabling* situation for him/her: the deaf child cannot communicate with the peers, the wheelchair-using child cannot fully join in their physical activities, the developmentally delayed youth cannot keep up with them intellectually.

4. *Media.* Perhaps the media do not show ethnic, gay, or female persons in proportion to their presence in the actual society, or in flattering ways, but they *do* reflect their presence; disabled people are rare indeed in television, movies, print, and sound media, newsworthy only when they are "super-crips" performing feats beyond the accomplishment of most *non-disabled* people, such as Rick Hansen, Terry Fox, and Steve Fonyo. Moreover, it is even more rare that the person portraying a disabled individual on television or in the movies is actually disabled him/herself:

witness Al Pacino as a blind man in *Scent of a Woman*, Tom Cruise as a wheelchair user in *Born on the Fourth of July*, or Alan Arkin as a Deaf person in *The Heart Is A Lonely Hunter*.

Clearly, there is a crucial difference not merely between marginalized groups and non-marginalized groups but also between disabled groups and groups who are marginalized for other reasons. Blacks, Jews, women, and visible minorities have suffered discriminatory treatment, persecution, enslavement, and even genocide, but they have always had a visible presence in the society. Disabled people, on the contrary, have been hidden away from public view. Even today there are still "normal" people who believe that those with visible disabilities such as paraplegia or cerebral palsy should be kept out of public sight, or who think of Sign language as "monkey talk" unfit for "civilized society". As pointed out above, disabled people have historically been squirrelled away in isolated schools and kept out of the media: they lived largely in hospitals or group homes, and worked either in sheltered workshops or in menial labour where they were unlikely to be seen by others (Nagler, 1990).

In 1992, a tentative exploration was undertaken of the repercussions of "differential" treatment upon the political socialization of disabled people (Roots, 1992). Perhaps not surprisingly, it was found that disabled people — even those actively involved in the overtly political disabled rights movement — felt themselves politically uneducated and inefficacious, unwelcomed by political parties and the state apparati, cynical, powerless, and culturally estranged from the political system. Their political orientations were similarly confused and unstable, and their ability to understand even simple political issues was questionable. While the differences in questions make it difficult to compare these survey results with those of other researchers who surveyed the general population, the overall negative and alienated findings of the research seem far more severe and extensive than those of "normal" people as surveyed by, for example, Goldfarb and Axworthy (1988), Clarke *et al.* (1991), and the *Vector Public Opinion Report* (1993).

Even among disabled people, the D/deaf are uniquely marginalized by virtue of the fact that theirs is a disability of communication, *both* orally and aurally (as distinct from those who, such as autistics, have a communication disability which is only verbal-expressive or cognitive). Whatever their exclusion from mainstream society, otherly-disabled people at least share the same language paradigm and the same biological media of communication, namely, voice and hearing. This is one of the reasons why capital-D Deaf people in fact do *not* view themselves as having a disability: they regard themselves instead as a cultural minority.

AGENCIES FOR EXAMINATION

Family (by which is generally intended "parents"), schools, peers, and media are universally recognized as the chief agencies of political socialization. They are by no means the only ones: post-secondary institutions, spouses, religious institutions and personnel, organizations such as the Boy Scouts or Girl Guides, and the military and "secondary organizations for adults" (including, presumably, one's workplace) are also important influences (Beck, 1977).

The focus of this book is upon the differences and similarities, not between disabled people and non-disabled people, or even between people who are deaf and people who have other disabilities, but only between the Signing Deaf and the oral deaf. The agencies which most conduce to these particular differences and similarities are the family and the schools, with the peer group being partially included as an element of the school's overall influence.

Before studying these agencies in their relationships to people who are deaf, it is necessary to review the historical, linguistic, and educational backgrounds of the D/deaf as these factors set the stage for their political socialization.

II

HISTORICAL OVERVIEW OF THE DEAF

HISTORY OF THE DEAF

ACCORDING TO GROCE (1985:99), "The earliest known written mention of deafness was in the Babylonian laws, which restricted the rights of those born deaf". From their first appearance in recorded history, then, people who are deaf have suffered deliberate discrimination and marginalization.

In his *History of Animals* (Book 4, chapter 9), Aristotle stated that speech and hearing form the conduit of thought, knowledge, and intelligence. Lane has argued (1984:91-92) that Aristotle actually described the link as an "accident" which did *not* mean intelligence was dependent upon hearing. Be that as it may, this statement, or its misinterpretation, has contributed immeasurably toward shaping the hearing world's negative perspective of deafness for more than two thousand years.

The Judeo-Christian religious tradition gave impetus to similar pejorative views. Talmudic laws from the second century BC restricted the legal rights and responsibilities of congenitally deaf citizens and ranked them with children and the mentally retarded (Silverman, 1970; Carver, 1988c). The Bible declares repeatedly that a person must *hear* the word of the Lord, and that faith in Jesus will "open the ears of the deaf and the mouths of the dumb". Saint Paul stated that "Faith comes through *hearing* the Word of God" (Romans 10), which Saint Augustine influentially interpreted literally to mean that "This impairment [i.e., deafness] prevents faith" (*Contra Julianum Pelagianum*, 3, 10).

Thus, myths stigmatizing and marginalizing "the deaf and dumb" were planted in pre-Christian laws, in the holy books, and in the seminal writings of Aristotle and Saint Augustine: those who could not hear or speak were as insentient animals, incapable of either reason or abstract ideas or memory, shut off from faith and forgiveness ... and therefore justifiably categorized as "not persons under the law" even in advanced civilizations, from Ancient Greece to Industrial England (Di Carlo, 1964; Lane, 1984).

A key document in the development of the manualist-oralist schism is the Justinian Code of the sixth century AD: it made a distinction between deaf and deafened people, curtailing the rights of the former with justifications that echoed Aristotle. The distinction was based upon deafened persons' continued ability to function in the oral-aural language of the society: unlike prelingually deaf people, they could usually still speak reasonably clearly and could use their memory of spoken words to develop lipreading skills.

It is apparent that the distinction codified by Justinian II inspired the propagation of similar distinctions and legal restrictions in subsequent eras, so that by the eighteenth century most states prohibited "deaf-mutes" from owning or inheriting property, marrying, voting, or acquiring an education (Groce, 1985:100). For the development of the manualist-oralist schism, the single most important of these proscriptions was the denial of the right of primogeniture where the prospective heir was "deaf and dumb". There appears to have been a fairly high incidence of deafness among the courtiers of Europe, possibly due to their inbreeding (Silverman, 1970); these noble families faced the loss of their titles and fortunes if their heirs could neither hear nor speak. According to Lane (1984), desperate aristocrats sought out any potential solution — even skull-cracking and head-drilling — to "unstop the ears" of their deaf child. When these pseudo-medical attempts failed, the parents were often willing to pay enormous sums of money for years of tutoring by those who professed to be able to teach the deaf to speak and lipread "well enough to pass for a hearing person". The nobles frequently set up entire private schools for the tutors, sometimes securing a charter and funding directly from the throne. This was the beginning of formal education for the deaf.

This development might reasonably be designated the point at which the division between manualists and oralists became institutionalized within the formal political socialization process (as distinct from the legal process). The goal of the oralists was to integrate nobles who were deaf, to train them to pass for hearing persons and thereby assume the full functions, rights, and responsibilities of a "normal" citizen of "normal" society. Such an objective necessitated putting as much distance as possible between the speaking-and-"hearing" noble and the nonspeaking-and-gesturing labourer, marginalizing the latter not merely for reasons of socio-economic class but for reasons of choice of communication mode (Groce, 1985). In the oralist rationale, then, the stigma of deafness *per se* was to be concentrated upon only the Signers: the simple fact that the latter could not or would not attempt to pass for hearing persons "proved" and *ipso facto* justified their legal, social, and political (and, it was believed, biological) inferiority (Markowicz, 1980:273-75).

The Abbé de l'Epée of France is credited with "discovering" the Deaf community of Paris, codifying their rough Sign language and studying its structure and principles, and opening the first school for the deaf that used Sign as its principal means of communication and teaching. In a felicitous irony, Epée opened his school in the decades of turmoil leading up to the French Revolution. As a religious personage his motive was not, of course, that of "the equality of men and of citizens"; it was concern that Deaf people must live and die in sin because they could not hear the Word of God. Canon law prohibited the Deaf even from celebrating mass "because they were unable to speak the words of the Eucharist required for the mystery of transubstantiation to take place" (Lane, 1984:92).

Epée's great importance is not limited to his advocacy of Sign and his educational methods. These two elements, along with his tireless championing of Deaf people and his genuine respect for them, created the crucible for Deaf self-awareness and socialization. The fact that "deaf-mutes" were not persons by law, had no rights, were considered ineducable and incapable of reason,[1] were in many places forbidden to associate with each other, and were deemed by religious fiat to have been condemned to a life of irrecoverable sinfulness followed by denial of entry into heaven must indeed have rendered them brute, isolated, incommunicado, and miserable (Sacks, 1989:13-14). By recognizing, codifying, and teaching their language, Epée gave them a means of communication and contact; by bringing them together in his school, he gave them a community and an identity; by means of language, knowledge, and community, he encouraged them to develop a culture and self-respect. In all of these developments, we can see the formal and structured socialization of the Deaf finally beginning to take effect, distinct from that of the oral deaf, for any such socialization requires

---

[1]   "As late as 1749 the French Academy of Sciences appointed a commission to determine whether deaf people were 'capable of reasoning' " (Dolnick, 1993:37).

language, community, and instruction — exactly what Epée's school provided.

Laurent Clerc, a graduate of Epée's school, was brought to the United States in 1816 by Thomas Hopkins Gallaudet to establish America's first Deaf School and to bring systematized Sign to Deaf Americans (Lane, 1984). His French Sign Language was blended with indigenous proto-ASL Sign languages to shape modern American Sign Language, which spread so quickly that the champions of the oral method took alarm. Epée's methods were simultaneously spread throughout Europe by his followers, successors, and Deaf students; they had the effect of generating pride in national Sign languages, encouraging the socializing of Deaf with Deaf, and nurturing Deaf Cultures. These developments were deeply perturbing to the oralists, who saw them as threats to their power and their livelihood and, less self-interestedly, as an affirmation of the deaf who persisted in using "barbaric gestures" and living in a Deaf ghetto when they were (in oral-ist theory) perfectly capable of learning to speak and to "hear" and to be properly socialized into a "normal" civilized status (Baynton, 1993).

The conflict between the advocates of Sign (mostly Deaf teachers) and the advocates of oralism (hearing educators, speech therapists, doc-tors, administrators, and the hearing parents of deaf children) came to a head at the Milan Congress of teachers of the deaf in 1880. This Congress was dominated by the hearing opponents of Sign language, who succeeded in passing a resolution proclaiming "the incontestable superiority of speech over sign for restoring the deaf-mute to society" (Lane, 1992:113, 115, 119). The effect of this resolution was to be almost beyond credibility.

AFTER MILAN

The Milan edict was immediately implemented in Deaf schools all over the world, and within a generation or two its "victory" was virtually total:

In America, there were 26 institutions for the education of deaf children in 1867, and ASL was the language of instruction in all; by 1907, there were 139 schools for deaf children, and ASL was allowed in none. The French figures provide a comparable glimpse of ruthless linguistic imperialism: in 1845, 160 schools for deaf children, with LSF [*Langue des Signes Française*] the accepted language; by the turn of the century, it was not allowed in a single French school. (Lane, 1992:113)

With Sign forbidden and the use of spoken language strictly enforced, non-oral Deaf teachers and school personnel were slowly driven from the field. Nearly half of American teachers of the Deaf had been Deaf themselves; within ten years the percentage had fallen to one quarter, and was down to one fifth by World War I, and had been reduced to just one tenth by 1990 (Lane, 1992:116).

The academic and occupational achievements of Deaf people declined in tandem with the loss of Deaf teachers and Sign-based instruction (Stokoe, 1980). This decline is literally visible in the business and casual correspondence and in the publications of, for example, the Canadian Association of the Deaf. Papers from its leaders — presumably the elite of the Deaf community — who were educated at Deaf schools up to the time of World War II reveal a formidable vocabulary and a perfect command of English with impeccable grammar, punctuation, and spelling. A study of papers produced by its leaders educated after World War II uncovers a Grade Three or Four level of literacy skills and an impoverished vocabulary. Carver (1988a) reported that the current rate of functional illiteracy among Deaf Canadians might be as high as 65 percent; he blamed this not on any lack of intelligence or capability of the Deaf themselves but on an educational system which, by denying them a natural language and culture within which they can function capably and comfortably, in effect socializes them into stupidity.

Important journals such as the *American Annals of the Deaf* frequently published erudite and influential research papers by accomplished Deaf scholars in the nineteenth century; these contributions disappear throughout the twentieth century (Andersson, 1994). From Epée's time until the Milan resolution, Deaf people held prestigious positions and jobs as educated professionals (Sacks, 1989); at the same time that Sign was banished, the Deaf schools were transformed from academic institutions into training schools for manual labour, streaming their students especially into the printing industry where their deafness was perceived to be an advantage in working the thunderous presses (Stokoe *et al.*, 1965:304-05; Schein, 1968:96). Such presses have become largely obsolete today, as have many of the semi-skilled jobs that the Deaf used to fill (Draper, 1992). The unemployment rate among Deaf Canadians in the 1990s is loosely estimated to be between 85 and 92 percent (Canadian Association of the Deaf, 1994d). Only 12 percent of Deaf school enrollees graduate from high school — in fact, until the 1950s there was not even a true high school for the Deaf in Canada (Beam, 1990:11)! Only 2 percent of Deaf Americans go on to university, compared to 40 percent of hearing Americans (Dolnick, 1993:40).

The connection between the Milan decree and today's astronomical unemployment and illiteracy rates for Deaf people may seem exaggerated until we turn to the study of the language of education and the socializing influence of the Deaf schools. These issues will be analyzed in the next chapter. To prepare for them, however, it is appropriate to review the history of languages used in the Deaf classroom since Milan.

THE LANGUAGES OF THE DEAF CLASSROOM

Outside of Quebec and a few francophone pockets in other provinces which use *Langue des Signes/Sourds du Quebec (LSQ)*, the language of Deaf people in Canada is basically American Sign Language (ASL). That Sign is the natural and most comfortable language for Deaf people has been recognized and indeed proven in numerous studies (Klima and Bellugi, 1979; Petitto and Marentette, 1991; Kannapell, 1993; Erting, 1994; McIntire, 1994; Petitto, 1994). It is also confirmed anecdotally by, ironically, oral successes such as Wright (1969), Kisor (1990), and Merker (1992), who write of their obsessively enrolling in refresher training in speech therapy and aural rehabilitation on a lifelong basis; there is no comparable account of Deaf persons obsessively enrolling in refresher Signing courses on a lifelong basis, because Sign is a *natural language* whereas oralism is an *acquired skill* and hence constantly in need of professional reinforcement ... as Kisor *et al.* admit, not in order to *upgrade* one's skill but merely to *minimize its inevitable deterioration over time.*

The banning of ASL from Deaf schools meant that a more or less totally oral methodology was in use for most of the twentieth century; in Canada, from about World War I to the 1970s (Carbin, 1996). Deaf people never ceased to furiously attack oralism, but the forced replacement of Deaf educators and administrators by hearing oralists meant they were voices on the outside without any power or influence on the inside (Beam, 1990; Lane, 1992).

The steady and precipitous decline in educational, social, and occupational achievements of Deaf people could not be denied or ignored forever. By the 1970s, attempts were being made to improve the receptive comprehension of Deaf students — without actually bowing to their need for ASL/LSQ — by developing some form of gestural cues that could augment oral methods (Glickman, 1984). Several such systems were developed: Signing Exact English, Seeing Essential English, Linguistics Of Visual English, and Cued Speech are probably the best-known ones. They are known generically as Manually Coded English (MCE). These are all sign *systems*, not Sign languages: they are constructs which avoid the unique grammar, syntax, and structure of ASL and instead codify English on the hands and mouth (Stokoe, 1980; Baker and Cokely, 1980). Deaf people consider them "ugly", "boring", "slow", "confusing", and almost impossible to master (Valli *et al.*, 1992; Kannapell, 1993; Solomon, 1994). Pinker (1994:39) has observed:

Educators at various points in history have tried to invent sign systems, sometimes based on the surrounding spoken language. But these crude creoles are always unlearnable, and when deaf children learn from them at all, they do so by converting them into much richer natural languages.

The results of experiments with these sign systems have been little better than those of a pure oral methodology; consequently, they have lost much of their popularity in North American schools for the Deaf.

For a brief period in the late 1970s and 1980s, Total Communication was the great educational hope. In retrospect, this hope seems misplaced, for Total Communication is not even a method but merely a philosophy (Erting, 1994). Its guiding principle is that the deaf child should be educated by whatever method might "work" for that individual: ASL, the various sign systems, oralism, technical aids, or any combination thereof. In practice, the decision on methodology was the teacher's to make, and quite naturally most teachers preferred to use the means with which *they*, not the child, were comfortable and in which *they* were competent. Since the teachers were nearly all hearing and thus largely incompetent in ASL, the selection of methodology usually turned out to be Manually Coded English or oralism plus technical aids, or Simultaneous Communication (SimCom) which consisted of speaking and adding a few MCE signs at the same time (Lane, 1992; Erting, 1994). Even those few teachers who were themselves Deaf Signers generally avoided using ASL in the classrooms, apparently under pressure of their administrators (Valli *et al.*, 1992; Kannapell, 1993).

The evident failures of the oral method, the various sign systems, and Total Communication still have not led to a revival of ASL in the schools. The chief reason seems to be simply that hearing people continue to control the decision-making process and remain understandably reluctant to adopt a methodology that would likely force their own withdrawal from the field (Lane, 1992). The root of animosity toward Sign itself is a socializing one: specifically, it is the hearing person's conceit that the world is a hearing world and society's language is a spoken and heard one, therefore the person who is deaf must become fluent in the dominant language in order to function in society and be a participating citizen (Glickman, 1994).

The current educational hope is a bilingual-bicultural approach, known as Bi-Bi. The radical difference of the Bi-Bi philosophy is that it was conceived and advocated by the Deaf themselves as "the Deaf community's answer to mainstreaming and an alternative to the trend in Deaf education for 'total communication'" (Solomon, 1994:43). Briefly, it insists on early language intervention to give the deaf child Sign as a natural and comfortable first-language as early and quickly as possible: the child will then have a linguistic base from which to acquire a second (oral-aural) language, which can be taught principally through writing. ASL should not only be the child's language of instruction but should be taught formally in the Deaf schools, just as English is taught formally in English-language schools. Fluency in ASL leads to the easier acquisition of English, a fact supported by numerous empirical studies proving that the Deaf children of ASL-using Deaf parents grow up to be more fluent in English than the Deaf children of non-Signing hearing parents (Meadow, 1968; Nash and Nash, 1981; Kyle and Woll, 1985; Dolnick, 1993; Andersson, 1994; Erting, 1994). The bicultural aspect, of course, involves the teaching of Deaf culture as equal to that of the dominant hearing culture (Mason, 1994).

The growing enthusiasm of the Deaf community for the Bilingual-Bicultural approach involves a profoundly serious concession on its part: Bi-Bi accepts that the ultimate aim of socialization should be a functional degree of integration into the dominant system, i.e., the hearing society. This is the overt goal of the oralist approach. Yet, convergence between the two philosophies cannot take place so long as Signers insist that the Deaf language and culture are necessary for the *personal* integration, identity, and self-actualization of the D/deaf individual, while oralists insist that Sign and Deaf Culture are a deviance and an admission of failure.

Approximately four schools in Canada have moved or are in the process of moving towards Bi-Bi as their methodology; however, this changeover has been in effect for only a few years and it is too soon for a definitive evaluation.[2] Most Deaf schools in Canada still utilize oral methods and technical aids in combination with either a sign system or Pidgin Signed English (PSE) (Vlug, 1995:10-14). The latter is a hybrid in which (generally-)ASL signs are used in (generally-)English word order, with a fair amount of flexibility in either direction (Baker and Cokely, 1980; Woodward and Markowicz, 1980).

MAINSTREAMING

Until the disabled rights movement of the past quarter century, a majority of disabled children were sent to residential schools designed for their particular disability. It was an act of segregation which usually involved accessible buildings and "appropriate" health care but also an inferior education and a deliberate streaming into menial occupations or sheltered workshops. Integration of disabled children into normal schools became one of the key demands of the rights movement (Driedger, 1989; Nagler, 1990; Barnes, 1991). Governments and school authorities responded positively, not only because the disabled advocates had convincing arguments but also because the special schools were expensive to run and were far from being cost effective: schools such as that of the blind in Halifax and of the Deaf in Amherst, with enrollments of 31 and 91 students respectively, cost $79,616 per pupil in 1993 (APSEA, 1994).

Signers were the only disabled group to fight *against* this push for "mainstreaming". The implementation of mainstreaming has been guided by the principle of setting "the least restrictive environment for the child". Deaf advocates pointed out that to pluck a deaf child from a Deaf school and put him/her among hearing peers with hearing teachers conducting lessons in oral-auditory language was in fact to place that child in the *most* restrictive environment (Brill, 1976). Even providing such a student with an interpreter is not equivalent to providing the least restrictive environment: there is little or no direct relationship between student and teacher, the student is subject to the physical and mental strains of staring in virtual immobility at one person (the interpreter) throughout the classroom sessions,[3] and the

[2] Solomon (1994:44) claims that in the United States, "The [Bi-Bi] system's successes are astonishing," but does not provide substantiation.
[3] These observations were made in Carol Patrie: "Educational Interpreting: Who Leads the Way?", *RID Views* (Registry of Interpreters for the Deaf), February 1994, and in Lane, 1992. They are quoted in "Starr", 1994:22, 24.

interpreter is seldom available outside of the classroom "when peers are left alone to build relationships with each other" (Stinson and Leigh, 1995:156). In addition, mainstreaming removes the child from a social environment with which he/she could identify and participate fully, and drops him/her into one which must remain alien and full of obstacles (Carver, 1988b; Mason, 1996).

Unfortunately, the present era is one in which governments at all levels are under tremendous pressure to reduce costs and to do what *appears* to be the "sensitive" thing, which in this case is universal mainstreaming. The R.J.D. Williams School for the Deaf in Saskatchewan was shut down in 1992 for these reasons; likewise, the Jericho Hill School in British Columbia was transplanted into the midst of a hearing school, and the Amherst School in Nova Scotia (serving three Maritime Provinces) was closed in 1995 (Lamont, 1994).

A study of the school as a political socializing agent for D/deaf persons, then, must include examination of two widely differing *kinds* of schools: the Deaf school and the hearing school. The former takes *only* D/deaf children[4] and utilizes some form of Sign language or sign system as both the language of education and the social language; the latter takes some Signing children and virtually all oral deaf or hard of hearing children, immerses them in a student body of hearing peers, and uses oral-aural English or French as both the educational and the social language.[5]

The hearing school can take a variety of approaches to the deaf student. There is some confusion even among researchers as to the distinction between "mainstreaming" and "integration". Mainstreaming refers to a group of deaf children who attend a hearing school but take most (though not all) of their classes together in segregated "labs" equipped with technical aids. Integration refers to one or more deaf child who take(s) all classes with hearing peers. The child may or may

---

[4] Special-needs classes for otherly-disabled children (usually either blind or developmentally disabled children) are sometimes located in a separate part of the buildings.

[5] "Early deafness is a low incidence handicap. The ratio is approximately one per one thousand children. With the typical proportional distribution of children, this means that only an occasional elementary [hearing] school would have as many as one child living in its district, and generally two or less living in the district served by any particular high school." (Brill, 1977:55) Note that Brill confines his statistics to *prelingually deaf* children and does not include those who became deaf between the ages o. five and fifteen.

not be provided with interpreters; if so provided, the interpreters likely use MCE or oral (silently repeating words on the lips without signing) translation. More often, though, the deaf child — whether Signing or oral — must depend solely upon technical aids and lipreading to function in the hearing classroom. Doe (1988:4) utilized the intriguing term "marginalized inclusion" to describe this situation. Lee (1992:160) added that even though it is called "integration", this is not true integration but rather is *assimilation* because it involves "one-way integration, forcing Deaf children to integrate with hearing children on hearing people's terms."

Despite their differences, Deaf schools and hearing schools share the goal of socializing deaf students into the hearing world. In this respect, of course, they could be said to be no different from the educational processing of the hearing child, but there are indeed important distinctions. The goal of enculturating the child to the specifically *hearing* society is obviously much more overt in the case of deaf children; and the attempt, unlike that for most hearing children, is at least partially doomed by the fact that the child simply is *not* hearing and therefore can never become fully enculturated. It is for this reason that Doe (1988:5) observes, "Marginalization is a process that results in the deaf being trained and expected to be part of hearing society while the barriers to full participation still remain."

DEAF CULTURE

For a long time, even the Deaf who used ASL as their first language internalized the assumption that it was something less than a "real" language (Schein, 1989:37-39). It was not until Stokoe published his linguistic research in the 1960s that either Deaf or hearing people began to realize ASL was in fact a true language (Stokoe, 1960; Klima and Bellugi, 1979; Stokoe, 1980; Kyle and Woll, 1985; Sacks, 1989). Subsequent psycho-social and linguistic studies developed the understanding that if Sign is a real language, then a real culture nurtures and is in turn nurtured by it: in Stokoe's term, language is simply "central in total culture" (1980:42).

The Deaf Culture is a primary socializing agent of Signers. It conveys and educates in the values, behaviours, and roles both of its members and of others, including the hearing society (Stevens, 1980:208-09).

The Deaf Culture has its heroes — people like Laurent Clerc and David Peikoff[6] — and its villains, such as Alexander Graham Bell, who urged the forced sterilization of all deaf people (Lane, 1984:356-59). It has a long and detailed legend, usually commencing with the Abbé de l'Epée and often turning upon the endless fight to preserve Sign.[7] Rutherford (1993) published a study of American Deaf folklore that includes apocryphal tales, jokes and stories, untranslatable puns and "Sign-play". Deaf sports leagues number in the thousands, and there are annual international conferences on Deaf history and an international Deaf clown festival. The National Theatre of the Deaf is world famous. The Silent Network is a satellite television channel whose flagship show, "Deaf Mosaic", won several Emmy Awards. The Deaf have their own insurance group (National Fraternal Society of the Deaf), nursing homes (Bob Rumball Centre for the Deaf in Toronto), and innumerable newsletters and magazines (Gannon, 1981; Carbin, 1996).

Schein (1989:64-66) lists some of the outstanding values of the Deaf culture: these include extremely strong school ties, a reverse categorization of degree of deafness (someone who is not profoundly deaf might be called "a little hard of hearing", whereas someone who is not very deaf at all might be called "very hard of hearing"), facial expressiveness (the "poker face" admired by hearing society is the communicative equivalent of a verbal monotone to a people who communicate visually), and a belief that no hand gesture should lack meaningfulness. Padden (1989:12-13) adds that staring is a necessary part of Deaf communication but is considered rude in hearing culture. She also points out that whereas hearing people respond to the introductory question, "Where are you from?" by naming their current city of residence, Deaf people answer with the name of their childhood home and their school.

Stokoe (1989:55) identifies the crucial "dimension of difference" between Deaf culture and hearing cultures as being "the use of vision

---

[6] Peikoff, who died in January 1995 at age 94, founded or co-founded at least two Deaf organizations including the Canadian Association of the Deaf; co-founded the Canadian Hearing Society; founded one school for the Deaf (Saskatchewan) and revived a second (Manitoba); established the Gallaudet University Alumni Association; and was the first Deaf person to have a university chair of studies named in his honour. He is most famous, however, for his astounding fundraising achievements on behalf of Deaf education.

[7] See, for example, Renate Fischer and Harlan Lane, eds.: *Looking Back* (Signum, Hamburg, 1993); and John Van Cleve, ed.: *Deaf History Unveiled* (Gallaudet University Press, Washington DC, 1993).

instead of hearing for getting [both] vital and incidental information". Padden and Humphries (1988:24, 38) underline the importance of this fact for the Deaf culture as a socializing agency: a culture is a system that explains things and how they can be known, and it also constrains things that can be known. The literature of the culture — its stories, legends, and folklore — not only passes on the community's history but teaches the wisdom of the group. In the case of Deaf people, it teaches them how to cope with and understand the hearing world. Thus, as Rutherford (1993:82) shows, Deaf storytellers explicate details that hearing audiences would consider unnecessary, because the former cannot assume the Deaf audience has acquired the same "repertoire of knowledge" and information that hearing people acquire through the radio, television, overheard conversation, and so on. It is for this reason that the Deaf culture prizes not the well-educated person but *the person with information.*

Like hearing society, Deaf culture has its rules and standards, and they include rules governing who belongs, who does not, and who deviates. Baker and Cokely (1980) designed a typology of Deaf Culture membership which identified the measurement of membership as being *attitudinal deafness.* Shorthanded within the community as simply "Attitude", it reduces the importance of *audiological deafness* as a prerequisite for acceptance. It is thus a rejection of the hearing society's pathological view of deafness in favour of a difference model. "This way of approaching deafness does not ignore the physical disability deafness imposes; rather it seeks to understand the way it canalizes and constrains social and cultural behaviour" (Erting, 1994:33).

Many hearing people still tend to assume that people who are deaf share the same language and culture as hearing society but are, by reason of their deafness, somewhat inferior in ability and intelligence (the Aristotlean legacy). This deficiency approach results in mapping the socialization methodology of hearing society upon people who are not hearing, an incongruity which can produce a diagnosis of deviance and a prescribed treatment aimed at normalization. For example, since the assumption is that people who are deaf share the language and culture of the hearing society, standardized tests designed for hearing children are given "as is" to deaf children (Lane, 1992:80-81). The culturally and linguistically different deaf child usually scores poorly and is assessed as "linguistically deficient", "culturally deprived", and even "retarded". The results of these tests are then published and used as guidelines in developing curricula and "treatment" for the deaf and in the training of those who will work with them, such as teachers, audiologists, and speech pathologists (Kannapell, 1993; Israelite, 1988).

The difference model is the exact opposite of the deficiency model: it assumes that people who are deaf share the same capabilities and intelligence as hearing people but have a different language and culture, which "canalizes" the individual to a differing socialization methodology. Assessments conducted on this basis disprove the pathological assumptions of intellectual inferiority and locate the root source of deaf people's difference/deviance in the issue of *communication* (Stokoe *et al.*, 1965; Stokoe, 1980; Kyle and Woll, 1985; Padden and Humphries, 1988; Carver, 1988a; Lee, 1992; Kannapell, 1993; Caselli, 1994; Erting, 1994).

The Deaf Culture's socialization, as hinted above, can be structured upon Baker and Cokely's typology of membership, in which Attitude is the floating determinant. The four elements of the typology are the Audiological (extent of hearing loss), the Political (holding of positions of responsibility within the Deaf community), the Linguistic (mastery of Sign), and the Social (participation in the social life and events of the local Deaf community). It can easily be seen that an oral deaf person cannot be considered a member of the Deaf Culture even though he/she may be as physically deaf as the proverbial post.

Baker and Cokely's typology of Deaf Culture, however, overlooks a very important shaper of attitude, membership, and socialization: namely, personal background. This category covers a number of factors which not only go far toward determining the acceptance of a Deaf person by the Deaf community but which also determine how *hearing society* will endeavour to socialize him/her to the dominant culture (Erting, 1994). These personal background factors include the following:

Parental deafness. Deaf children of Deaf parents are a rare phenomenon: only 10 percent of the Deaf populace have Deaf parents. The benefits within the Deaf community of such a heritage are considerable, akin to that of being "first citizens" (Solomon, 1994:40).

Age of onset. Prelingually deaf persons are the "true Deaf" — for better in the Deaf Culture, for worse in the hearing culture, because of the difficulty prelingual deafness creates for acquiring oral language skills but the ease it creates for mastering Sign.

School attended. The Deaf culture, identity, and language is incubated and transmitted in the Deaf schools. Attendance at such a school has traditionally been all but mandatory for acceptance, although that is now softening in recognition of the spread of mainstreaming.

Extent of education. In almost no other marginalized group is so little value attached to the extent of one's education, and seldom is the attainment of educational distinction such a cause for suspicions as to one's loyalty to the community (Higgins, 1980:55-57). The reason for this distrust may rest in the perception that Deaf graduates and professionals are successful *to the extent that they conform to the values of the hearing world* (Doe, 1988:135, 137). Such a conformity suggests rejection of the Deaf world, or at best, questionable Attitude toward the latter, and incomplete Deaf socialization or enculturation.

This overview of the membership requirements of Deaf Culture highlights serious discrepancies between the deaf child's reality and the expectations of the two main agencies of early political socialization, i.e., family and school. The deafness of a child disrupts his/her relationship with his/her hearing family; the Deaf attitude toward education and choice of school is deviant from that of hearing society and family members. This may explain why the political socialization agendae of these two agencies seem often to be still driven principally by the historical motivations of oralism, i.e., the determination to deny or eliminate the deafness itself along with its effects, and to prevent or delay the deaf child's "defection" to the Deaf Culture. These two factors become the primary objectives of political socialization; the *standard* socializing goal of integrating the individual into the norms, values, and behaviours of the society becomes *secondary*.

This, in turn, suggests further answers to the question of why *both* oralist and manualist approaches to the socialization of deaf children generally result not in integration but in marginalization. It is not simply a matter of society's attitudes toward stigma, or society's obstacles to the full participation of persons who are different, or even the physical reality of deafness — although it does involve all of those factors. It is something more which involves the assumptions and operating precepts of political socialization and its agencies. We will attempt to achieve a clearer understanding of this question in the following chapter.

III

SOCIALIZING AGENCIES

THE FAMILY

Diagnosis and Parental Reaction

THE ASSUMPTION of the socialization literature is that there will be some easy linguistic means of communication between parents and child; indeed, this is the assumption which hearing parents make, too. But 90 percent of deaf children are born to hearing parents who, moreover, have very likely never before known a deaf person (Schein and Delk, 1974:35-36). The birth of a deaf baby therefore delivers three very great shocks to the parents. One shock is the diagnosis of deafness itself. Another shock is the realization that their own experiences of socialization will almost certainly be largely inapplicable to a deaf child. A third shock is "the absence of a common — that is, a spoken — linguistic system" (Meadow-Orlans, 1987:30).

Natural feelings of guilt and inadequacy which accompany these shocks are exacerbated by the often protracted struggle to confirm the child's deafness. Meadow-Orlans describes case histories in which parents who suspected that something was wrong with their child's hearing were repeatedly told by medical professionals that they were mistaken, incompetent, and even stupid (1987:31-32). When the diagnosis of deafness is finally confirmed, the parents slowly come to realize that they are unable to influence the child's destiny, i.e., to "undo" the deafness (Schlesinger, 1985; Carver and Rodda, 1987; see also Wright, 1969, for an autobiographical account). It is common for parents to confess that this process leaves them feeling as though their child has died and been replaced with an inferior being who has no future or who has had his/her range of life choices truncated (Nash and Nash, 1987:107; Kisor, 1990:15; Dolnick, 1993:46; Erting, 1994:91-92).

Normal parental expectations for their child, and the blow to those expectations from the discovery of deafness, carry a great influence upon the nature and tone of the family's approach to socializing him/her (Erting, 1994:19). For example, the parents tend to play less with the deaf child and to interact with him/her in a more extreme manner: dominant-possessive, passive-indulgent, smothering or aloof. Warren and Hasenstab (1986:292-93) explain that while parents undoubtedly want to do what is best for the child, "accepting a child with a severe hearing impairment is difficult". Becker (1987:61) goes so far as to claim that the emotional bonding between parent and child which normally accompanies the socialization process is often lost. Meadow-Orlans (1987:37) concludes, "Clearly, it is difficult for parents to engage in normal socializing behavior when they are deeply concerned and depressed about the health and normal development of their infant."

It is not only the health and development of their infant that interferes with the parents' socializing behaviour: it is also the realization that received socialization processes cannot be utilized "as is" with deaf children. For one thing, the sheer alienness of a deaf individual deprives the parents of "a major guide to child-rearing — their empathetic reactions" (Schein, 1989:111). Secondly, the deafness of the child has the effect of a completely unexpected attack upon the hearing parents' own identity and selfhood, because language is the most important content and instrument of socialization and is therefore inextricably part of a person's selfhood (Erting, 1994:1). For hearing parents, themselves socialized by means of a spoken language, being a speaker of a language is fundamental to their understanding of themselves and their social world. Dolnick (1993:38) adds:

But the crucial issue is that hearing parent and deaf child don't share a means of communication. Deaf children cannot grasp their parents' spoken language, and hearing parents are unlikely to know sign language. Communication is not a gift automatically bestowed in infancy but an acquisition gained only by labourious effort.

The third reason received socialization procedures are rendered irrelevant or ineffectual is because, as noted above, they are rooted in the assumption that *all* involved parties — the society itself, the socializing agencies, and the child — share a common language, which in modern Western society is invariably an oral-aural language. Where one of the parties does not fit this paradigm, it will be in tension with the other two parties. Usually, of course, it is the deaf child who will be the party out of synch. Where the child is fortunate enough to be the one in ten who is born to Deaf parents, however, it is the society that is at odds with the child and the primary socializing agency, i.e., the parents. Not coincidentally, this "Deaf-of-Deaf" child will generally develop into a strikingly more accomplished and politically efficacious individual than either the oral or the Signing D/deaf child of hearing parents (Stuckless and Birch, 1966; Vernon and Koh, 1970; Brasel and Quigley, 1977; Stokoe and Battison, 1981; Ivers, 1995; Meadow-Orlans, 1987; Erting, 1994). These more positive achievements are directly attributable to the fact that the Deaf parents share the deaf child's language and culture and are therefore able to socialize him/her on a mutually compatible and appropriate basis. These children are comparable to post-lingually deafened persons who, as hearing children,

were involved in family decisions making. They learned the process early in life. Thus, they grew up feeling they could influence and control what happened to them in life. Most adults who were born deaf were denied this opportunity [because they had hearing parents]. The few congenitally deaf leaders ... generally had deaf parents. Thus, they were able to participate in their family life and in the [D]eaf community. They learned from this what leadership requires. (Vernon and Estes, 1975:4)

Warren and Hasenstab (1986:293) observe that the deaf child's ability to develop self-esteem depends upon his/her ability to communicate and upon the family's attitude toward him/her; if the former is upset, the latter is likely to be upset also, leading to poor self-esteem. Poor self-esteem, in turn, leads to feelings of political inefficacy and indifference, and unsuccessful political socialization (Rosenberg, 1962).

Language Choice as Political Choice

How to bridge the communication gap between a prelingually deaf child and his/her hearing parents in order to socialize the child? It is the parents' unenviable task to decide between two modes of communication — oral and Sign. The choice is certainly not an easy one.

The family may not in fact view the choice as being primarily between language modes but rather as a choice between keeping the child in the family or surrendering him/her to an unfamiliar culture with which the hearing family members can never identify. The natural parental impulse is to declare that the family is the best place for a child; but as we have seen, the hearing family is stripped of its socialization expertise in this case, it faces an almost insuperable communication barrier, and its confidence in its ability to deal with the child's deafness is likely to have been badly shaken by the diagnostic experience.

The choice of language for the deaf child is not only a choice of communication mode or of cultural identity: it is a political choice as well, in two different perspectives.

One perspective concerns Easton's systems persistence model of political socialization. The fact that the majority of hearing parents and practically all professionals (doctors, audiologists, and so on) tend to identify the primary challenge of deafness as *integrating the child into "the hearing world"* would appear to confirm the influence of the persistence model of socialization. The child's deafness is diagnosed as a threat to the process of aggregating children into the existing overarching social structure because that process is rooted in oral-aural means of transmission and it utilizes parental knowledge and experience for its implementation. Integration requires the *repairing* of the relevancy of these two instruments via the tools of oralism; their *replacement* by Sign and the Deaf Culture — "foreign" instruments to the dominant social structure — would logically lead to "foreign" or deviant results, and deviance means marginalization.[1] The systems persistence model, then, is one of the strongest motivating forces for adopting the oralist path for the deaf child.

The second perspective in which language choice is political choice pertains to power, particularly within the politics of the family. Prelingually deaf children can acquire language through only one channel: visually. The natural *visual* language of a human being is manual-gestural: studies such as those of Petitto and Marentette (1991) have established that the born-deaf child babbles manually at the same stage and at the same rate as hearing children babble vocally, *regardless of whether his/her parents talk or sign to him/her.*[2] The question is whether

---

[1]   See, for example, the arguments of A.G. Bell on these points as reported in Van Cleve, 1993:341. Bell stressed that forcibly integrating (socializing) the deaf child into the hearing world through oralism must be held even more important and more urgent than the child's academic achievement.

[2]   Groce (1985:54) claims that "some research indicates that the ability to sign may in fact precede the ability to speak by several months." See also Bellugi and Klima, 1972; McIntire, 1977; Caselli, 1994. Notoya *et al.* (1994) reported that acquisition of Sign occurs more quickly than oral-language acquisition.

the hearing parents of a deaf infant choose to build the language acquisition process upon this natural mode of expression/reception or whether they will choose instead to attempt to map their own linguistic preferences upon the child.

The choice of Sign is a granting to the child of political power within the family: it acknowledges *and accepts* his/her difference and uniqueness *vis à vis* the other members of the family. The family structure adjusts to the child. On the other hand, the choice of spoken language, regardless of whether by means of pure oralism or by some form of Manual Coding, denies the child political power and manifests a refusal to accept his/her difference. The child is forced to adjust to the family structure.

"Normalization" versus "Managing Difference"

The choice of oralism is a denial of more than the child's political power within the family: it involves the entire family in a denial of the child's very deafness as part of the process of "normalization". Professionals such as speech therapists and aural rehabilitation workers insist that for oralism to succeed, the family must constantly talk to the child, force him/her to respond vocally, and never fall back upon even basic human gestures except as a last resort. Ladd (1990b:48) criticizes this approach as "equating the normality of behaviour [with] normality of speech." Schein (1987:205) adds poignantly, "'Normal' for many Deaf people is a passive form of rejection", upon which Kannapell (1980:113) elaborates:

To reject a language is to reject the person herself or himself. Thus, to reject ASL is to reject the Deaf person. Remember ASL is a personal creation of Deaf persons as a group. Perhaps those hearing or Deaf people who cannot deal with ASL are really saying they cannot deal with or accept the Deaf person. (1980: 113)

Acceptance of difference constitutes the (Deaf) cultural model; denial of difference (oralism) constitutes the deficience model. Deficience treats deafness as a deviance, a stigma. Hence, ironically, the choice of oralism as the best hope of integrating the deaf child actually reinforces the very stigmatizing aspect of deafness that *prevents* integration.

Manualism manages difference by "culturalizing" it. Deafness as a cultural attribute (rather than as a physical handicap) is similar to, say,

Blackness or Jewishness in that it may yet retain its stigmatized or deviant character in the eyes of the dominant society, but it cannot be considered a deficience; *ipso facto*, prejudicial treatment by the dominant society manifests a situation of social inequality rather than personal inferiority. To thus move the location of the "problem" from one's own deafness to society's inequities is to politicize it and consequently to present motivation and opportunities for the Deaf person to gain some power over his/her own destiny (Fine and Asch, 1990; Bickenbach, 1993). In contrast, to insist as oralism does that the problem is firmly located in one's deafness (or rather — and significantly — one's "*hearing* impairment") is to medicalize it and to deliver control of the D/deaf person's destiny into the hands of others such as doctors and audiologists.

Power Relationships and the Pattern of Marginalization

The victory of oralism at the 1880 Milan Congress coincided with medical and technological developments that at first appeared to promise both cures for and prevention of deafness: Bell, after all, invented the telephone in the pursuit of an amplification device for the deaf, and by the turn of the century doctors were becoming increasingly sophisticated in their understanding of the causes and prevention of deafness. The ascendency of oralism dovetailed with these developments to construct a web of interests aimed at the integration of people who are deaf. Lamont (1994:3), for example, lists 13 different professions delivering direct services to a deaf student! Lane (1992) classifies these and related professions (along with oralist hearing parents) as "the audist establishment", estimates its value in the United States at $2 billion, and claims it is almost entirely composed of hearing people. Rutherford (1993:5) echoes: "The rise of the Oral Method brought a decline in self-determination for Deaf people and an impingement of their language by decision-makers outside of the Deaf community and the Deaf experience."

The point here is that there is a tremendous power differential within the political context in which D/deaf and hearing people interact: simply put, "Hearing people have a great deal of power over deaf people's lives" (Erting, 1994:71). The difficulties of communicating with the prelingually deaf child moves these hearing people to utilize their power ("power resides implicitly in the other's dependency" [Emerson, 1962:32]) to make decisions for the deaf person, thereby (intentionally or not) infantilizing him/her, and consequently socializing him/her into a passive and dependent role — into "learned helplessness" (Baker-Shenk, 1985). McCartney's (1986) survey of oral deaf adult members of the strictly oralist Alexander Graham Bell Association For the Deaf reveals that these self-identified "oral successes" placed greatest value upon those "components of oralist items" that are in fact parent-directed (e.g., "My parents taught me manners"), while their parents placed greatest value upon those components that evidence parental control over the deaf child's life decisions (e.g., hearing aids, early auditory training, use of residual hearing). McCartney concluded that oral deaf adults succeed not so much through their own efforts or preferences as through a value system that is instilled by their parents and teachers: "Were it not for parents' and teachers' values, the hearing-impaired child might not [even] have the desire to be oral" (136, 141).

This is not to suggest that in most cases there is a deliberate and malicious plot to disempower the person who is deaf: on the contrary, most hearing people (particularly parents) have only the best of intentions. As Carver (1988a:73) points out, however, they themselves: "may be as much victims of the 'system' as their deaf [subjects] are. That is, instead of being oppressors themselves, they more probably are instruments of oppression without their realizing it. The 'system' in question is the society's perception of deafness".

Freire (1970:150) traces the subtle way in which this structure of interests moves into a situation of what he calls "cultural invasion": "The invaders penetrate the cultural context of another group, in disrespect of the latter's potentialities; they impose their own view of the world upon those they invade and inhibit the creativity of the invaded by curbing their expression [i.e., their language]".

Lane's (1992) term for this "cultural invasion" is "colonialization", since he sees "the audist establishment" as a structure of hearing interests exploiting the D/deaf for their own benefits (including their economic benefits — recall the $2 billion dollar value he affixes to their activities). He goes so far as to equate oralism with political violence: the parental choice of oral-aural language over Sign disempowers the child of his/her most basic and essential element of identity, of function, and even of *thought* itself (because language is believed to be a prerequisite for cognition), and forces upon him/her instead an unnatural language which uses an unfamiliar mode and an inaccessible channel of communication. This sets up a pattern by which parents make choices for the deaf child on the assumption that he/she is a marginalized figure within even the familial politics, a situation Woolley (1992:90) describes as follows:

Deaf people are often criticized for their apathy and for not taking initiative but no one ever gives them a chance. They have been denied the right to take part in decision making ever since mummy and daddy and brother and sister got together and decided to go to the seaside for the day and then told the Deaf child to eat her breakfast and get ready to go out somewhere.

This kind of generic situation would distress Hyman (1959), for his review of political socialization literature elicits the clear conclusion that a child must be able to believe he/she has some real political power within his/her immediate relationships if he/she is to grow up with political interests and a sense of efficacy. Elkin (1960) and Greenstein (1965) further remind us that the child's relationships with his/her family form a major determinant of how he/she learns to relate to others, including the society's political system. Schlesinger (1986, 1987) notes that the hearing parents of deaf children feel powerless — a feeling reinforced by their dependence upon professionals for guidance — and they pass this condition onto their deaf child (i.e., powerless parents raise powerless children), whereas Deaf parents in the same context have the knowledge and confidence that come from first-hand experience with deafness and hence prove to be powerful parents, and consequently capable of giving power and autonomy to their Deaf child.

The pattern of marginalization established in hearing family politics thus conditions the deaf child to expect the same hearing-paternalistic treatment in other spheres. The child grows up believing he/she has neither the power nor the ability to make decisions, to influence others, to argue a point of view, to negotiate and compromise: in fact, he/she may never even be granted the opportunity to learn how the process of decision-making is conducted (Erting, 1994:56).

A Particular Oralist Identity Problem: The Tensions of Realities

In most cases, the child is probably a willing participant in the oralist process of denying the deafness. We are reminded by Greenstein (1965:79-81) that the first 13 years of life are a period of "great plasticity and receptivity" during which the child not only learns uncritically (and depends almost unquestioningly upon the parents for information, guidance, and decisions) but also develops the "experiential filter" that screens out certain segments of reality that do not seem to fit into the socio-cultural environment of his/her family. In the oralist family, one such ill-fitting segment of reality is the fact that the child is not and never can be a hearing person.

As the deaf individual grows and becomes aware that in fact he/she cannot hear, a tension is set up between his/her actual deafness and the "hearing" identity created for him/her by the family and other authority figures such as doctors, therapists, and educators.[3] As Nash and Nash (1987:116) put it: "For the deaf family member, the archival sense of self he or she may acquire in the context of family life is very fragile, and more likely to be challenged when that person engages in interaction outside the family."

In Dawson's terms, this early socialization has failed to teach the child where he/she properly fits in the "social category system" (1977:44) or what his/her social identity is: hearing and integrated? hearing and marginalized? deaf and integrated? deaf and marginalized? Parental attempts to "save" the child from the latter category create a credibility gap between the goal of "hearingness" and the inescapable fact of deafness. The oral deaf youngster may rationalize this credibility gap by attributing his/her difficulties in speaking and lipreading to his/her own "stupidity" simply because, under the oralist doctrine, it cannot be due to deafness. In Goffman's terms, this child has acquired identity standards which he/she applies to him/herself in spite of failing to conform to them (or rather, in spite of their inherent inapplicability), with the inevitable consequence of self-estrangement, ambivalence as to his/her own identity, and problems with self-esteem and the sense of efficacy (1963:106).

A Particular Manualist Identity Problem: The Splitting of the Family

One of the major reasons hearing parents choose the oral method over Sign is the fear of "losing" their child to the Deaf world (Dolnick,

---

[3]   Charrow and Wilbur (1989:103) limn the sub-stage of this transition. Prelingually deaf children do not know what hearing is; "It is only when they [are] required to look, perform, behave, and achieve like hearing children that they begin to see themselves as 'not normal' — as opposed to merely deaf." In other words, they become aware of their stigmatized status *before* they become aware of the stigma itself.

1993:51-52). Sign is definitely the key to this other world, and unfortunately it is a key that hearing family members will normally never be able to fully grasp even if they themselves attempt to learn Sign and to educate themselves about Deaf Culture (Erting, 1994:30). Moreover, those hearing parents who choose Sign, especially if they also choose to have their child educated at a centralized Deaf school, knowingly transfer much of their own crucial socialization responsibilities to the school and the peer group, where Sign is the language of normality and deafness is no handicap. It is a confirmation for them of the loss of control over the child that they first felt when the diagnosis of deafness was made.

Some analysts, such as Schein (1987) and Kannapell (1993), seem to imply that if parents do not adopt Sign for their deaf child, the child will drift toward it anyway as an adult. Schein, for instance, claims, "The Deaf community stands *in loco parentis.* As substitute parent, it can fill a void in the lives of the majority of deaf children" (1987:131). He seems to suggest that the fact that 90 percent of deaf children are born to hearing parents *inevitably* results in family estrangement; parental choice of Sign for the child only lessens the degree of hostility within the estrangement. Other writers, such as Erting (1994), Kluwin and Gaustad (1994), and Woolley, Ladd, Lee, and others published in Lee (1992), assure that even if Sign is a struggle for parents and siblings, their choice of manualism for the deaf child and their own efforts to learn some Sign are sufficient to enable the deaf child to feel a part of the family: "The atmosphere can be relaxing as [manualism] releases the family's emotional pressure simply by lessening the strain on the mechanics of understanding" (Ladd, 1992a:38). This assertion seems disingenuous. It would be more accurate to observe that instead of "lessening the strain on the mechanics of understanding", Sign simply shifts the power base of familial communications, placing the greater strain of understanding upon the hearing members, whereas oral communication places the strain primarily upon the deaf member.

In any case, the feelings of helplessness and mourning that hearing parents first felt upon the discovery of deafness persist or return with the realization that their Deaf child will largely identify with what to them is an incontrovertibly alien culture and language. Erting (1994:5) argues that while such feelings are normal, they are essentially self-blaming in nature, and for most families the blame should not be inwardly directed:

The fact that even family members who have strong emotional bonds with the deaf individual behave in ways that reveal their very basic lack of understanding of the deaf experience, sometimes in spite of extraordinary efforts at understanding and accommodating, confirms the deaf individual's belief that only other deaf people can really understand or behave appropriately.

The forces propelling deaf individuals toward community with other deaf people exist in opposition to the dependence and family ties moving them in the direction of mainstream hearing-speaking society.

The struggle is the deaf person's to undertake, and it is not an easy one. Erting defines it as a conflict between the individual's *social* identity (the need for community with those who share one's communication mode and experiences) and *personal* identity (the parent-child bond); the struggle results in ambivalent attitudes and yearnings between the Deaf culture and the hearing culture.

THE SCHOOLS AND PEER GROUP

Choices

As discussed in chapter 2, the choice of schooling can be divided into two camps — oralism or manualism — but this division is somewhat arbitrary because *all* currently utilized methods of educating the deaf are oral; only the degree of permissible subsidiary manualism varies. The true alternative to oralism — Sign *alone* — is not an available educational option for Deaf Canadians and has not been so since shortly after the 1880 Milan Congress.

This does not mean hearing schools are interchangable with Deaf schools. The latter uniquely offer Deaf peer groups, Deaf culture, Deaf identity, Deaf role-models, and an atmosphere where manual communication is the norm at best or tolerated at worst. Hearing schools, on the other hand, offer the opportunity to interact on a daily basis with the dominant hearing society, and they offer probably a more challenging curriculum and academic standards (Meadow-Orlans, 1987:45). These differences are crucial elements of the differing socialization processes, goals, and results of oral and Signing deaf students.

Hearing parents generally cannot be expected to choose knowledgeably among school options. Not being Signers themselves, or at best having limited ability to judge the Signing skills of others, they may not realize the teachers in the Deaf schools are not communicating effectively with the students, or that the interpreters in the hearing schools are labouring in a similarly unsatisfactory arrangement. The deaf child him/herself may not know or be able to articulate his/her preferences.

Additionally, the hearing parents tend to be swayed by facsimilies and/or approximations of "normalness". In the former case, integration into a hearing school "makes a declaration of normalcy: see, Dick/Jane goes to the same school with all the other children in the neighbourhood" (Schein, 1989:112). The parents might measure approximations of normalness by the amount of school time devoted to "deafness treatment": speech therapy, aural rehabilitation, and so on. A fully integrated deaf student, for example, may strike them as being "closer to normal" in that he/she usually takes the regular hearing curriculum plus occasional one-to-one sessions with an itinerant special education teacher or speech therapist. Compare this to a mainstreamed student, who could find 20 to 40 percent of the school day devoted to speech and hearing "labs" or to deaf-only classes, and to a student in a Deaf school, who could spend from 40 to 80 percent of the time in such remedial classes and in MCE training sessions, always in the company of other Deaf students only (Lane, 1984; Jacobs, 1989; Schein, 1989; Dolnick, 1993; Canadian Association of the Deaf, 1994b; Erting, 1994). Such variations in "deafness treatment" and in the amount of time devoted to academic subjects pose a real dilemma for the parents who wish to give their deaf child both effective communication skills and an effective education: the two objectives appear to almost cancel each other out as far as the schools are concerned.

The School as a Reinforcer of Orientations

The child comes to the school with attitudes and orientations that have been shaped by the family. Greenstein (1965) and others believe that the school's initial essential function is to reinforce these attitudes or to correct them if necessary, and to extend them to institutions and relationships beyond the family nucleus.

Thus, if the deaf child has been marginalized from the politics of the family and/or made to believe that failure to pass as a "fake hearing person" means failure as an acceptable social being, the school will almost inevitably confirm and reinforce those concepts regardless of whether it is a Deaf school or a hearing school. Similarly, if the child is placed in a Deaf school only as a last resort — that is, only after he/she has been enrolled in hearing schools and "proven" unable to cope — he/she is labelled an "oral failure"; this process (which unfortunately remains the one currently in use throughout Canada) not only marks the child for life as a "failure" but also unfairly contributes to the low academic standards (and reputations) of the Deaf schools.

The deaf child who has been integrated into the family as a *Deaf* person (because his/her parents are themselves Deaf) is more likely to have his/her self-confidence and self-identity reinforced by the Deaf schools acting as an extension of the Deaf family; it is no coincidence that the four student leaders of the "Gallaudet Revolution" of 1988[4] were all "Deaf of Deaf" and graduates of Deaf schools (Gannon, 1989; Dolnick, 1993). If that same Deaf-of-Deaf child is mainstreamed or integrated, however, his/her self-identity will be placed under attack by the school because acceptance of one's deafness is "incorrect" according to the norms of the dominant (hearing) society which uses the hearing school as its socializing and conforming agent (Kannapell, 1986; Valli, 1992; "Starr", 1994).

Environmental Concerns

Most schools make few environmental concessions to the realities of prelingual deafness. The Deaf school will usually provide certain physical modifications to accommodate the special needs of the child, for example horseshoe-shaped desk arrangements to enable the child to see his/her classmates in addition to the teacher at all times; the hearing school will not provide this minimal accessibility for isolated deaf students except as an accident of the teacher's personal preferences for classroom seating arrangements.

Carver *et al.* (1991) provided a formidable catalogue of other environmental considerations which are frequently overlooked by Deaf schools and which are certainly rarely if ever brought to the attention of hearing schools. These include: plain walls and draperies (patterns and bright colours are hard on the eyes of visually oriented students); soft yet thorough lighting (to minimize both glare and shadows which

---

[4] Gallaudet students went on strike, shut down the university, and became a worldwide top media story as they protested against the appointment of a hearing person as the school's president. They made four demands, including the appointment of a Deaf president, and won all of them. See Gannon (1989) for a complete account, and Sacks (1989) for an interesting outsider's version of the events.

interfere with lipreading and Sign-reading); absorbent ceiling tiles (to eliminate acoustic reverberations that reduce the effectiveness of hearing aids); and thin carpet rather than bare floor tiles (for better sensitivity to vibratory clues).

Role Models

Hearing schools offer no Deaf role models such as teachers and administrators; most Deaf schools offer only a few Deaf employees in lesser positions such as dormitory supervisors and janitors. Lack of positive role models confirms for the student the marginalization of people who are deaf. It forces deaf students to adopt hearing role models with whom they cannot truly identify. It can also create or reinforce already-formed misconceptions such as the very common belief of deaf children that they will become hearing persons when they grow up.

The Deaf child of Deaf parents can usually compensate for the school's lack of role models through his/her parents' Deaf friends and acquaintances (and of course the parents themselves) and through their awareness of and interest in less immediate Deaf models such as the actress Marlee Matlin, the university president I. King Jordan, and the politician Gary Malkowski. Most hearing parents do not have Deaf acquaintances; and while they may seek out Deaf role models such as Malkowski for their child, their own inability to identify with such models can prove awkward and make their professed admiration seem forced and insincere.

Recent research by Doe (1996) provides an interesting illustration of the above argument. Comparing Deaf women with hearing women, she found that in both cases the choice of positive role models was shaped by a shared communication mode: "Hearing women named mothers and other adults as role models while Deaf women named peers or teachers at schools" (48). This obliquely parallels some of the findings of the research for this book; oral deaf — so-called "fake hearing" — people tend to admire and defer to their parents and other adult power-figures, whereas Signers tend to follow the examples of their peers or the few Deaf staff at their schools.

Language Challenge

The oral student in the hearing school struggles with a strange language, one he/she cannot hear and can speak only with considerable difficulty: namely, an oral-aural language such as English or French.

The Signing student in the Deaf school, oddly enough, is not particularly better off in the classroom because the language of instruction is usually a manual codification of the dominant spoken language. Gee and Goodhart (1994:232-33) and Erting (1994:26) point out that this awkwardness extends even to those children who are Deaf-of-Deaf and fluent ASL users from infancy: they arrive at school to find their ASL being "corrected" by non-fluent hearing teachers who press MCE upon them. Such a situation can not only confuse and oppress the Deaf child but can also fuel an antagonistic relationship between the child and the school which will be carried over to his/her relationship with the hearing society. The rejection of a child's usual means of communication serves to communicate rejection to the child (Erting, *ibid*).

Impact upon Political Learning

The points raised in the three sections above are not insignificant for the political socialization of deaf children because, as Greenstein observes, "In *political* socialization research it is especially important to take account of the setting in which learning takes place" (1965:167; italics in original). Children are expected to mature socially within the educational system. Dawson is at pains to emphasize that "acquiring a political self is a corollary to general social maturation" and that "political learning seems to coincide with other types of social learning. Political identities are formed during the same period when other social identities [i.e., one's 'social category'] are acquired" (1977:42, 60). The deaf child in *any* kind of school — Deaf or hearing — receives a clear if occasionally subliminal message from the institution and its functionaries that he/she is inferior, has non-standard environmental needs that will not be met, suffers unusual language handicaps which will not be accommodated, and carries a stigma with which few if any within the system will identity and which few (as a role model) can guide him/her to accept and "manage" in Goffman's sense of the term.

This pervasive negative message impacts upon the four forms of direct political learning that Dawson (1977:105) has identified as being assigned to the schools for delivery: imitation, anticipatory political socialization, political education, and political experiences. Who is the deaf student to imitate but hearing peers or role models, who obviously cannot teach him/her to deal with his/her deafness? Anticipatory political socialization involves anticipating powerlessness and inferiority as hearing people make decisions for the deaf student and treat him/her as a "substandard" human being, and as that deaf student sees either no other deaf people at all or else deaf people only in menial positions. As for political education and experiences, Roots (1992) has shown that deaf students are excluded from or provided with nugatory training in these two aspects of political socialization: most Deaf schools in Canada do not have student councils, none have classes in political science, and overt political education can consist solely of a visit to the parliament buildings. All of this has led to the frequently expressed and somewhat bitter opinion of Deaf Canadians that "Politics are for hearies" (i.e., hearing persons).

Internalization of Diffuse Support

Easton and Dennis (1969) hypothesized that the principal political socialization role played by the school is to internalize diffuse support for the existing system: that is, to ensure that the bond between the citizen and the authoritative institutions is strongly positive from an early stage in life so that it will persist passively throughout adulthood. The school utilizes four functions in pursuit of this goal: politicization, personalization, idealization, and institutionalization.

Politicization sees the school acting as the transitional agency between the family and the "structure of political authority" (391). But the latter is "for hearies only": it is an alien and aloof nebulosity which functions in an inaccessible language and communicative mode. The oral child may cope by indeed accepting it as a continuation of the paternalistic and infantilizing presence of familial authorities; the Signing child is more likely to regard it as an extension of the alienation experienced within his/her family, i.e., as another institution with which he/she can find only formal common ground because of linguistic and cultural discrepancies.

The school curriculum is intended to *personalize* political authority by giving it concrete form, for example in the immediate figure of the principal and the more distant figure of the prime minister. This sets up a situation similar to that of the role models within the school itself: with the sole exception of Gary Malkowski, there are no D/deaf political authorities — at least not in the view of the schools or the hearing world. In real life there are potential ones: the leaders within the Deaf community. Since the Deaf world is a "deviant" world, however, the schools are more likely to view its political authorities (for example, the President of the Canadian Association of the Deaf) as threats to the existing order or as irrelevant, rather than as acceptable personifications of authority.

Trust in existing political authorities is encouraged through an *idealized* presentation of them. For a deaf child, actually, *any* hearing authority is an idealization, because the stress placed upon overcoming his/her "hearing handicap" sets hearingness as the ideal. The oral deaf child may indeed develop trust in the worthiness of hearing authorities simply because the latter *are* hearing, and also of course because he/she has trusted the parents who have established hearingness as the child's ultimate goal in life. The Signing deaf child, in contrast, develops a profound *distrust* of hearing authorities as he/she becomes enfolded more and more deeply into the Deaf Culture of the peer group.

Institutionalization — the transferring of positive feelings about personalized political authorities to political institutions — is the crucial last step toward inculcating diffuse support. If the *personalization* function has succeeded, the *institutionalization* function is also likely to succeed. As we have seen, however, personalization is very problematic for deaf children.

The oral deaf child who does personalize political authority must choose hearing authorities — he/she knows of, and is presented with, no others — and submits to them in a manner consistent with his/her lifelong pattern of infantilization. As stated earlier, the schools reinforce such attitudes and extend them to political authorities, confirming in the oral deaf child both his/her infantilized status and his/her passive trust in hearing authorities. This may qualify as "successful" political socialization, but it is surely a deformed success because the end product is an individual who gives passive support to political institutions within which he/she is marginalized and cannot properly function (because of the communication barriers), and with whose authorities he/she cannot identify. In fact, the "successfully" socialized oral deaf individual displays all the varieties of alienation identified by Seeman (1975): powerlessness, meaninglessness, normlessness, cultural estrangement, self-estrangement, and social isolation. Yet, superficially at least, he/she does grant trust and support to existing political authorities. Furthermore, the success of his/her integration is judged not by normal standards of political socialization but by the fact that he/she uses the society's standard communication methods, i.e., oral-aural language rather than Sign.

The personalization stage, on the other hand, is often the dawning of awareness for the Signing child of the real power distinctions between deaf and hearing people. Dawson (1977:42, 60) insists that political category learning occurs simultaneously with social category learning and that both occur during the early and middle school years, when the peer group becomes one of the strongest influences upon the individual: this is when the Deaf individual realizes that the standard political authorities are all hearing and alien to him/her. The authorities become externalized and remote from the Deaf person; identification with them is lost or damaged, and this loss of identification may be accompanied by a loss of trust in them, a recognition that "they do not represent *my* interests, *my* world". It may be at this early yet critical stage in personal development and maturation that the political socialization of the Signing child may be said to have arrived at failure in that the child rejects conventional society and embraces the Deaf Culture, rejects "marginalized inclusion" (Doe, 1988:4) and chooses full inclusion in a marginalized group.

Social Maturation and Peer Groups

Zweibel, Meadow, and Dyssegaard (1986) found that teachers described their deaf students as dependent, quick to give up, expectant of failure, demanding of attention, and requiring a disproportionate share of the teacher's time: in short, as highly immature. Significantly, these characteristics were found to be most pronounced in oral deaf children and less prevalent in Deaf-of-Deaf Signing children.

The latter's greater social maturation may be due to the important roles they play in the Deaf school's social life. They are the natural ASL Signers, and in the dormitories and playgrounds they become the teachers of the language to the children of hearing parents; they also assume responsibility for transmitting the Deaf Culture to their schoolmates (Higgins, 1980; Padden and Humphries, 1988). In fact, they are themselves the primary socializing agents of their deaf-of-hearing-parents fellows.

One possible reason for the greater immaturity of oral deaf children is that their internalization of inapplicable standards is intensified by their relationship with their hearing peers. Langton (1970:156) has identified the foremost function of a peer group as the transmission and reinforcement of the culture of the dominant society, which to a deaf person means hearing society. Inclusive school policies send the message that "for deaf students to be 'social successes' they must 'make it' with hearing peers, and that socializing with deaf peers is a mark of failure" (Stinson and Leigh, 1995:158). The deaf student at a Deaf school, of course, has a peer group whose foremost function is to social-ize him/her into the *deviant* culture. Woodward (1989:170) explains this latter phenomenon as the logical outgrowth of the D/deaf child's family relationships:

> Because most Deaf children have not normally had a refuge in the home from [hearing] cultural oppression, they appear at a very young age to have formed very strong ethnic ties with their peer group to cope with outside threats against self-concept and identity ... [This] may be one of the chief strategies for coping with an essentially hostile environment that is not often overcome with much help from parents.

Woodward's observations closely echo Eisenstadt's (1962:35-36) explanation of the role of "youth groups" in political socialization:

> Youth's tendency to coalesce in such groups is rooted in the fact that participation in the family became insufficient for developing full identity or full social maturity, and that the roles learned in the family did not constitute an adequate basis for developing such identity and participation. In the youth groups the adolescent seeks some framework for the development and crystallization of his identity, for the attainment of personal autonomy, and for his effective transition into the adult world.

Peer Group Attitudes

It is common for hearing parents to favour mainstreaming or integra-tion for their deaf children on the assumption that it will better prepare them for the hearing world. They see the "normal" school as an ideal agency for socializing the deaf child because it will compel him/her to (1) continuously practice oral-aural communication, and (2) socialize with hearing peers on the latter's terms (rather than on *equal* terms). Oral successes such as Wright (1969) and Kisor (1990) confirm the relentless oral practice. The socializing, however, is problematic.

Levitt and Cohen's (1976) research has shown that non-disabled children develop a negative attitude toward disabled children at school-entry age, that this attitude not only persists but intensifies as they grow older, and that contact with disabled children not only does not miti-gate the negativity but may intensify it: as Goffman muses, "familiari-ty need not reduce contempt" (1963:52). Loeb and Sarigiani (1986:98) and Stinson and Leigh (1995:157) confirm the applicability of this analysis to deaf students.

Langton's (1970) study of peer group influence on the political socialization of Jamaican students suggests one reason for these negative attitudes: homogeneous peer groups tend to reinforce existing cleavages that mark out "different" individuals as deviates or "discredited" members. Consequent rejection by one's classmates increases the deviant child's sense of isolation, self-dislike, and inferiority (Meadow, 1969; Loeb and Sarigiani, 1986; Meadow-Orlans, 1987:45; "Starr", 1994:20-21).

Not to be overlooked is the applicability of LaMare's observations on integrated Spanish-speaking Mexican-Americans (1974). He found that students who persisted in speaking Spanish were regarded by their English-speaking peers (both Anglo- and Mexican-American) as definitely inferior and undeserving of full citizenship privileges. The resultant tension between the groups contributed measurably to the Spanish-speakers' lack of political awareness, involvement, support, and efficacy. The diary of "Starr" (1994) indicates parallel experiences with mainstreamed deaf children. Ivers (1995:466) explicates that the disdain of the hearing peer group may be rooted in the fact that deafness is a hidden handicap and is therefore perceived by the non-deaf peers to be easier to overcome than visible handicaps; failure to do so "justifies" ridicule of the deaf child. This is especially true where the child inadvertently plays to these expectations by doing everything in his/her power to "pass" as a hearing person by speaking and "listening"; Merker, who is late-deafened but considers herself an oral success, reflects with telling irony on these external expectations: "My major disability is not my deafness; it is that I speak well, am an excellent lipreader" (1992:184). The damage done by the ridicule of peers to the deaf child's self-esteem, and his perceived inability to adapt to his environment, can lead to feelings of political inefficacy (Rosenberg, 1962; White, 1968).

At the opposite (i.e., positive) pole, Groce (1985) found that in Martha's Vineyard, where a significant percentage of the populace was genetically deaf until the twentieth century, the knowledge and use of Sign by *both* deaf and hearing people created a true linguistic equality which empowered the Deaf to be politically efficacious (to the point of holding elected offices) *and* fully integrated in every facet of life — social, economic, familial, administrative, and even military. "There was no language barrier and, by extension, there seems to have been no social barrier" (75).

An interesting parallel was found by Dean and Nettles (1987), Cohen (1969), and Weinstein (1968), each of whom recorded instances of "reverse mainstreaming" in which a few hearing children were integrated into a largely "hearing impaired" (oral deaf) classroom. In each case, the oral deaf students were noted to have benefited not only linguistically but in leadership abilities and self-sufficiency from the presence of *the minority group* of hearing peers. Evidently the deaf students' own status as the majority group conduced to a relaxed, confident atmosphere in which they were capable of absorbing whatever of value the minority group had to offer them without the impediment of feelings of inferiority, even though the oralist objectives of the educators meant the deaf students *still* had to defer to their hearing peers and let them (the minority group) set the standards by which achievement was to be measured.[5] It should be noted that the "hearing impaired" students (evidently clandestinely) utilized some "gestural language", much to the disapproval of the oralist teachers and researchers. In fact, Dean and Nettles noted that one hearing student began adopting the deaf childrens' "gestural forms of communication" instead of encouraging them to use their oral skills; rather than recognize this as an indication of the naturalness and ease of visual-gestural language for *both* deaf and hearing children, they dogmatically conclude: "This type of occurrence illustrates the importance of having at least two normal-hearing children in each class to provide examples of spoken language and conversation. It also points to the responsibility of the teacher to foster speech and language development" (32).

Elkin (1960:66) observed that the peer group provides the individual with a "comforting cushion in the face of demands of authority", but it can also increase the sense of social isolation. The Deaf peer group fills both of these roles powerfully: after all, the Deaf *are* isolated from mainstream society by virtue of their stigma, hence the act of becoming a member of the group and depending upon it for comfort and support must reinforce the child's awareness of the stigma and of the difference between Deaf Culture and hearing society. Peer group membership stresses the Deaf society's distinguishing characteristics, special interests, unique language, and idiosyncratic behaviour patterns

[5] Van Cleve (1993:335) describes the pioneering effort at reverse mainstreaming that was offered by David Barlett at his private school in New York and Connecticut from 1852 to 1861; according to a contemporary account, it was a great success, with perfect equality between Deaf and hearing students. Unfortunately, as a private school it ended up closing for lack of funds.

and values, sharpening the contrast with hearing society's characteristics and forcing the deaf child to a fuller realization of his/her own difference (Padden and Humphries, 1988). Politically, this is the engendering of Deaf "identity politics", in which, according to Elshtain, "the citizen gives way before the aggrieved member of a self-defined group" (1993:52). Elshtain deplores this development; but given the physical and attitudinal barriers that prevent the successful socialization of a deaf individual into conventional citizenship, perhaps membership in a self-defined group and a "politicized ontology" are a valid political option.

Quality and Ends of Education

Parents often choose to mainstream their deaf child in the belief that the quality of a "normal" education will be superior to that offered by the centralized school for the deaf. Several studies confirm this belief by demonstrating that the Deaf schools fail to equip their students with sufficient academic skills to compete with their hearing peers (Gentile and DiFrancesca, 1969; Meadow, 1980). There is doubt, however, whether these results stem from the actual quality of the Deaf schools' curricula and teachers or from cultural and linguistic incompatibilities. Erting (1994:20) blames the failure of the Deaf schools to "take account of the sociocultural aspects of deafness and their implications for education". The Canadian Association of the Deaf attributes it to "inappropriate educational methodology", that is, oralism and Manually Coded English (Canadian Association of the Deaf, 1994b).

Loeb and Sarigiani's findings indicate that deaf children may locate their specific academic weaknesses not in their own inherent abilities or in the school *per se* but rather in the obstacles they face on account of their deafness; for example, their "linguistic deprivation" [*sic*] makes it difficult for them to read well or to give a good oral report (1986:96). Bodner-Johnson (1985) rooted the deaf student's academic achievements (specifically reading and mathematics) not so much in the schools as in the family's acceptance and accommodation of the deafness, to the extent of including SimCom or ASL in the household and including the Deaf community as "an integral part of their lives"; in short, she identified the crucial element in scholastic success as the *family's* cultural and linguistic adaptation to the child's deafness (134-35).

At least two studies (Reich, Hambleton, and Houdin, 1977; Loeb and Sarigiani, 1986) confirm better academic achievement for mainstreamed students, but at the cost of greater personal and social problems. Nash and Nash (1987:113) note that the academic performance of mainstreamed deaf students is still below the average for hearing students; they also elaborate that while the deaf students "are present in the same building with hearing students, they are socially and culturally separate from the majority of students". If the education offered by the Deaf schools is of questionable quality because it is essentially remedial in nature, then the education offered by the hearing schools is of questionable quality because it is essentially inaccessible to deaf students.

Regardless of whether a school uses the oral method or Sign, it tends to expect less of deaf students than of hearing students simply because of their deafness; this becomes a self-fulfilling prophecy (Kannapell, 1993). Indeed, one review of Teacher Training Programs in Canada cited by Carver (1988c:88) concluded that teachers of the deaf are programmed to undereducate their pupils. Kyle and Woll (1985:268) found that deaf students may be promoted with undeserved good marks because they "try hard in spite of their deafness". There is consequently little motivation to learn, improve, or succeed; little meaningful reward for success or penalty for failure; and little training in the ability to recognize that development and improvement is a possibility in life in general.

The expectation of failure that infects the education of deaf children extends to the school's responsibility to prepare the student for employment. Many Deaf schools actively discourage their students' interest in ambitious careers: a student at the Amherst School in Nova Scotia complained that her dream of becoming an astronomer was mocked by teachers who refused to assist her because "deaf people don't need to know astronomy".[6] Students are routinely streamed into vocational training and discouraged from aiming at university and professional careers. This attitude is not irrelevant to the political socialization of the students: Zureik and Pike (1978:34) reported that "occupation expectancy is shown to be a powerful predictor of the sense of political competence."

The subsequent sections of this book, which report and analyze the results of a small survey of oral deaf and Signing Deaf adults, demonstrate the astuteness of this last observation.

---

[6] "Deaf-learning [sic] system slammed", *Halifax Daily News*, 30 January 1989, p.3.

unduly favouring the oral deaf, who invariably stay at home and attend nearby schools, in contrast to the Signers, who may be boarded out to distant Deaf schools.

A number of other questions were utilized to probe more subtly into the family situation. Primary among these were language and identity questions.

The Signers were found to persist in their preference for Sign, unchanged since childhood. The oral deaf subjects, on the other hand, had almost entirely abandoned the pure oralism in which they had been trained: they now tended to favour SimCom (Simultaneous Communication), which uses Pidgin Signed English or Manually Coded English in addition to speech, lipreading, and technical aids. When among their families, however, they reverted to pure oralism, continuing their lifelong pattern of adapting to the communication preferences of hearing authority figures. The Signers refused to resort to pure oralist methods with their families, even where their family members had no knowledge of Sign; they utilized SimCom or pen-and-paper communication where their Signing could not be understood. Their unwillingness to use oral methods probably confirms their weaker family ties but may also confirm their self-confidence in insisting upon "differential" treatment rather than "deficience/denial" treatment from their families; or it may simply reflect less confidence in their oral skills.

Another indicator of family relations is the persistence of attitudes toward oralism and manualism. The oral deaf individuals considered themselves part of the hearing world, and the Signing individuals considered themselves part of the Deaf Culture. These are predictable results, but they also substantiate hearing parents' fears of "losing" their Signing child to the Deaf Culture.

Upon further probing, intriguing differences are found in the interviewees' *rationales* for their adherence to their respective cultures. The oral deaf subjects reiterated the arguments they had received since infancy from their *hearing parents*: deaf people must live in the hearing world and therefore must speak and "hear", and Sign language and Deaf Culture are isolating and indicate a certain degree of inferiority (failure). The Signing subjects repeated the arguments they had received from their *Deaf peers*: oral deaf people are victimized into being "fake hearing people", and the deaf person's true happiness can only be found in Sign language and Deaf Culture. It is interesting to note that the Signers did not blame the oral deaf themselves for the sins of oralism but insisted they were the victims of "the audist establishment", which included their well-intentioned but misguided or poorly informed hearing parents.

POLITICAL OPINION, PARTICIPATION, AND ACTIVITY

The oral deaf subjects adopt the same political orientations as their parents, whom they cite as having the greatest influence upon their opinions; the Signing subjects do not adopt their parents' orientations and credit their (Deaf) friends as the greatest influence on their politics. Both instances confirm Hyman's (1959) conclusion that political orientations must be learned early in life if they are to persist: the oral deaf learned as infants from their parents and follow the same path in adulthood; the Signers, receiving their primary political socialization from their peers instead of from their parents, hold orientations in adulthood that often conflict with those of their parents but complement those of their socializing peers.

All but two members of each group recalled no direct political experience in school, and all but the same four individuals agreed they had received nothing worthwhile in the way of formal political education. The two Signing exceptions had both been involved in student councils, while the two oral deaf exceptions had both created semi-political organizations while at university. Equally pertinent is the question of whether these four exceptions *persisted* in their political interests: the two oral deaf were inactive within a couple of years of graduation, but the two Signers continued to be involved in Deaf political arenae.

A dearth of scholastic political education and experience is believed to lead to feelings of political inefficacy (Hyman, 1959). Setting aside the four exceptional individuals who naturally enough believed themselves efficacious, this hypothesis is confirmed with the oral deaf subjects but is decisively repudiated by the Signing subjects, all of whom felt they could make a difference in the political landscape and all but one of whom were involved in Deaf political issues.

The reasons cited by the oral deaf for their lack of efficacy were typical of hearing people: politicians are out of touch, one vote cannot make a difference, politics are corrupt, and so on. The Signers repeated the oft-heard assertion of Deaf Culture that "politics are for hearies," yet they do not appear to have allowed this opinion to negatively affect their faith in their own political efficacy.

Traditional "hearing" political instruments such as party memberships or contributions were entirely shunned by the oral deaf subjects; the Signing subjects indicated a greater level of involvement, but in most cases this was explicitly connected with the position of Gary Malkowski, the Deaf Ontario politician. Where activities did *not* take the form of mainstream or "insider" activity, however, the Signers and the oral deaf were at opposite extremes: *all* of the Signers had participated in public rallies, and *none* of the oral deaf had done so. Furthermore, the Signers' involvement was no one-time thing: all of them had participated in at least three rallies between 1988 and 1994. The oral deaf had never participated in any public political rallies.

This section of the questionnaire seemed to indicate that while the oral deaf and the Signing Deaf share the same lack of formal political education and experience in the schools, the oral deaf are nevertheless aggregated into the passive support for existing political systems which most political socialization analysts agree is a primary goal of the socialization process. The Signers, on the other hand, appear to subsequently overcome their lack of training and lack of early interest to become politically active.

COCHLEAR IMPLANTS: ATTITUDES AND ACTIVITIES

As might be expected from Lane's (1992) linking of cochlear implants with oralism, the device has polarized oral and Signing D/deaf people. This polarization is reflected in the results of our comparative study: all of the oral subjects supported cochlear implants for deaf children, and all but two of the Signers were opposed (the two exceptions, moreover, were ambivalent rather than supportive). All of the oral subjects indicated that their families shared their support for the implants; all but one of the Signing subjects stated that their parents held views opposite to theirs, i.e., their parents supported the implants (the eighth said her parents could not make up their minds on the issue). Again, then, the oral subjects have echoed their parents whereas the Signing subjects have conflicted with theirs.

All of the Signers had taken political action to make their opposition to the implants public: they had participated in the rallies, requested interviews with the media, picketed politicians, and written letters. These are activities characteristic of political *outsiders*. The oral deaf had maintained their uninvolved stance politically, with the lone exception of one individual whose only activity was to write a column in a magazine; the significance of this exception will become apparent below.

A formidable letter-writing campaign and pro-implant media coverage had fought back against the Deaf anti-implant protests; if the oral deaf people themselves had not been involved in these pro-implant activities, who had? According to the study (and corroborated by contemporaneous media reports), pro-implant activities were almost entirely carried out by *hearing people* — mostly parents and the medical professionals who "treat" deafness. Using personal meetings, letters, "friends in high places", powerful lobbyists, sympathetic civil servants, media manipulation (in some cases the activists held positions on editorial boards), and other pressure tactics, these groups rallied Ontario politicians and bureaucrats to defeat Malkowski's bid to block funding. The one oral deaf person in the survey who had written a magazine column on the topic admitted that her parents had not only pressured her to write it but had also instructed her on what points to include in it. In personal interviews, Health Canada officials indicated that pressure by cochlear implant doctors, implant hospitals, medical associations, device manufacturers, and parent groups such as Voice For Hearing Impaired Children (a strict oralist parent group) had led to the department's decision to allow the implants in children; moreover, the Deaf rallies had led to an organized avalanche of pro-implant letters to the department from parents.

A COROLLARY OBSERVATION

The subjects for the above study were selected on the basis of factors mentioned earlier, one of which was that they should all be gainfully employed on a full- or nearly full-time basis. At the time of selection, these were the only employment-related requirements; the choice of actual professions was random and indifferently noted. It was not until long after the interviews had been completed and analyzed that it was noticed that thirteen of the sixteen subjects are working *in the Deaf community* rather than in the mainstream community.[2]

---

[2] Of the other three subjects, one worked for his hearing father (is nepotism the only reliable way to attain employment in the hearing world?); one is unemployed despite his postgraduate level of education and abundant social skills (does the fact that he is "Deaf-of-Deaf" and a Signer suggest employer discrimination?); and one is self-employed as a logical extension of his extreme rejection of hearing peers and hearing/oralist schools.

Their profitable working integration into the hearing world, regardless of whether they were raised within the oral or the manual system, thus appears to be more chimerical than real. Are they working in the Deaf community because it is the only kind of job they can obtain, or because they are most truly comfortable only among other D/deaf people whether they realize it or not? Does the hearing world reject them as potential employees because, despite years of training in integration, they are still perceived first and last as people who are deaf and therefore deficient?

Equally noteworthy is the fact that these thirteen subjects are generally stuck in low-level positions despite their often impressive educational achievements and their proximity to middle age. The two factors suggest a lack of advancement in the workplace that may be attributable to a "glass ceiling" — an assumption that D/deaf people cannot function at a senior manager or executive level because of concerns about their perceived communicative limitations.

The lack of rigourous controls on selecting subjects for study by occupation prohibits the drawing of definitive conclusions; it is suggested only that employment appears to be a variable that tends to support the contention of this book that oral deaf persons and Signing persons *both* end up marginalized regardless of the methodology used to socialize them; for they *both* end up working in the Deaf community.

APPENDIX: THE QUESTIONNAIRE AND RESPONSES

Comparative Group Study Results

Interviews were conducted at various locations across Canada throughout the summer and fall of 1994.

Demographics: Sixteen individuals were interviewed: eight oral deaf subjects and eight Signing deaf subjects. Each group was composed of four women and four men. Fourteen of the individuals were in their middle-late thirties; one male in each of the two groups was in his mid-twenties.

All subjects were born deaf or prelingually deafened, and were the only deaf members of their immediate family.

Of the oral deaf, six grew up and still live in southern Ontario; the other two grew up and live in Western Canada. Of the manualists, three grew up and live in southern Ontario, one grew up in the West and now lives in the Maritimes, one grew up in the West and still lives there, and two grew up in the Maritimes where one still resides while the other now lives in Toronto.

Education. All of the oral deaf subjects attended mainstreamed or integrated classes and all relied totally upon oral methods of communication throughout their school years. The Signers were a more mixed lot: three were mainstreamed but used Sign from early in life; two attended Deaf schools where ASL was banned from classrooms (though clandestinely practiced in the dormitories and student areas); one started education in a mainstreamed environment, was labelled an "oral failure", and completed secondary education at a Deaf school; and two attended Deaf schools where they attained skill in both ASL and oral methods.

All members of both groups graduated from high school, and all but one Signer went on to university; a second Signer left university after one year. Those two men who are in their mid-twenties are both presently still undergraduates.

Employment. All but one individual are employed to some extent, most of them in professional occupations such as teachers or social workers.

The Sampling. The educational and employment status of the respondents may not be typical of the D/deaf populace, given the low rates at which the latter attend postsecondary education and attain full employment; whatever typicalness has been sacrificed in those areas is intended to be compensated by the equality of circumstances between the subjects, making comparison between them more fair.

The survey of 200 Deaf Canadians undertaken by Roots (1992) exposed the formidable difficulties of administering conventional questionnaires to Deaf people. It was decided to circumvent these problems in the present study by conducting casual interviews. In order to elicit true responses, the subjects were not informed that their responses were being recorded; it was explained that the interviewer was working on a study and was interested in their feedback and experiences with respect to the subject matter. They were aware, therefore, that their responses might be indirectly reflected in the subsequent report.

The hypothesis of the research reflected that of this book, namely: **"For deaf children, language choice (oral versus Sign) determines the course and tenor of the process of political socialization; both processes result in marginalization, but in different forms and extents of marginalization."**

PART ONE: FAMILY RELATIONS AND LANGUAGE/IDENTITY FACTORS

1. **How would you describe your relationship with your family members, particularly your parents: very close, close, acceptable, not very good, poor, hostile?**

	ORAL DEAF	SIGNING DEAF
Very close	5	0
Close	0	3
Acceptable	2	3
Not very good	1	0
Poor	0	1
Hostile	0	1

Note: The three Signers who described the relationship as "close" were the three individuals who were mainstreamed with Sign language interpretation.

2. **What are your *current* language preferences?**

ORAL DEAF

First preference:
Simultaneous Communication - 8

Second preference:
PSE or MCE - 4
Pure oral methods - 3
Pen-and-paper - 1

Third preference:
Interpreters - 4
Pure oral methods - 4

0 preferred Sign language, explaining that (with one exception) they had no skill in ASL.

SIGNING DEAF

First preference:
Sign language - 8

Second preference:
Interpreters - 8

Third preference:
Pen-and-paper - 4
PSE or MCE - 3
SimCom - 1
0 preferred pure oral methods.

3. What communication methods do you use with your family members?

ORAL DEAF

8 used pure oral methods.

8 used SimCom as their
second preference.

SIGNING DEAF

8 used Sign language.

4 used SimCom as their
second preference.
2 used interpreters as their
second preference.
2 used pen-and-paper as their
second preference.

3 used SimCom as their
third preference.
3 used PSE or MCE as a
third preference.
1 used pen-and-paper as a
third preference.
1 used interpreters as a
third preference.

0 preferred pure oral methods.

All insisted they would not
use anything else with their
families, even as a third
preference.

All stated they would rather
use interpreters as a second
preference but that this was
impractical.

4. Are most of your friends hearing, oral deaf, or Signing Deaf?

	ORAL DEAF	SIGNING DEAF
Hearing:	6	2
Oral deaf:	2	1
Signing Deaf:	0	5

5. Which culture do you consider yourself to belong to now: hearing or Deaf?

	ORAL DEAF	SIGNING DEAF
Hearing:	8	0
Deaf:	0	8

6(a). Why do you support/oppose oralism?

ORAL DEAF (support)

- deaf people must live in the hearing world; you have to be able to speak and understand speech in hearing society
- don't know any Signers
- better education and employment if you can speak

SIGNING DEAF (oppose)

- oralism tries to make deaf people into fake hearing people
- not my culture
- hearing people try to force us to be like them; let us be ourselves!
- cannot learn speech and/or lipreading
- oralism makes me feel uncomfortable, feel under constant pressure, stressful, frustrating

6(b). Why do you support/oppose manualism?

ORAL DEAF (oppose)

- only Deaf people Sign; it is not a common language
- marks you as different (i.e., a Signer cannot "pass")
- isolates you from general society
- only deaf people who can't learn oral communication need Sign (i.e., oral failures)
- not a real language

SIGNING DEAF (support)

- Sign is beautiful and natural
- it is my language, the only one I am comfortable with
- true Deaf identity is in Sign and Deaf Culture

PART TWO: POLITICAL OPINION, PARTICIPATION,
AND ACTIVITY

7. Did you vote in the 1992 Charlottetown Accord Referendum?

	ORAL DEAF	SIGNING DEAF
Yes:	7	8
No:	1	0

8. Did you vote in the 1993 federal election?

	ORAL DEAF	SIGNING DEAF
Yes:	5	7
No:	3	1

9. To the best of your knowledge, do you vote the same preferences as your parents? For example, do you vote for the same political party?

	ORAL DEAF	SIGNING DEAF
Yes:	7	2
No:	1*	6

* This individual volunteered the explanation that voting differences with his parents were inconsistent: he and they had voted the same in 1988; the father, mother, and son had all voted for different parties in the 1990 Ontario election; they all voted the same in the 1992 referendum; the mother and son voted similarly to each other but differently from the father in the 1993 federal election.

10. Who influences you the most in forming your political opinions? Choose one only.

	ORAL DEAF	SIGNING DEAF
Family	6	1
Friends	1	6
Media	1	1

Co-workers	0	0
Teachers	0	0
Professionals	0	0
Organizations	0	0

11(a). Were you involved in political activities at your school? If so, how?

ORAL DEAF

Only two subjects answered affirmatively: one helped establish a disabled students' lobby group, the other became president of a deaf and hard of hearing national youth organization.

SIGNING DEAF

Only two subjects answered affirmatively: both had been involved in their student councils, one as president. The latter also studied political science as his university undergraduate major.

11(b). If you were involved politically in school, are you still involved in political activities now?

ORAL DEAF

No (2).

SIGNING DEAF

Yes (2): active in Deaf political issues and organizations.

12. Did you receive any formal political education in school, such as "Civics" classes?

ORAL DEAF

Six had taken classes called "Civics", "Canadian Studies", or "The World Around Us"; none of the eight felt they had learned anything worthwhile about politics except for basic information about the Canadian Parliamentary system.

SIGNING DEAF

Three had taken the same kind of "Civics" class as the oral deafs; none of the eight felt they had learned anything worthwhile.

13. Do you consider yourself politically efficacious? Why or why not?

ORAL DEAF

Three answered affirmatively: two of these were the individuals who had been politically active in school.

Reasons for feelings of inefficacy:
- politicians are out of touch
- one vote cannot make a difference
- politics is corrupt
- ordinary people have no voice or power

Reasons for feelings of efficacy:
- advocacy work does make a difference
- government must listen to voters

SIGNING DEAF

All eight individuals answered affirmatively.

Reasons for feelings of efficacy:
- advocacy work does make a difference
- provide information to government
- hearing politicians know nothing about Deaf issues, therefore they have to listen to us when we talk to them (we educate them and influence them)
- our issues affect others besides Deaf people, e.g., senior citizens
- our votes make a difference

14. Have you participated in any of the following political activities recently, i.e., in the past two years?

	ORAL DEAF	SIGNING DEAF
Joined political party	0	2
Contributed to party	0	4**
Election campaign work	0	4***
Public rallies	0	8
Wrote/phoned politicians	2*	4***
Lobbied politicians	2*	3***

  * Same two people in these categories.
  ** Includes the two individuals who had joined a party.
*** All of these activities were directly connected with Gary Malkowski, Deaf politician in Ontario.

15. **If you checked anything in the previous question, have you participated in those same activities for a *longer* period of time than just the past two years?**

ORAL DEAF

No, in all cases above except one person who had been writing to politicians "since 1990".

SIGNING DEAF

Yes, in all cases above. Most activities could been traced back to 1990, around the time of Malkowski's election. However, participation in public rallies could be traced back to the 1988 National Deaf Education Day rallies for all eight respondents.

PART THREE: COCHLEAR IMPLANTS

16. **Do you support cochlear implants for deaf children?**

	ORAL DEAF	SIGNING DEAF
Yes:	8	0
No:	0	6
Not sure:	0	2

17. **Have you participated in any activities related to the cochlear implants controversy? If so, what?**

ORAL DEAF

Yes: 1
No: 7

SIGNING DEAF

Yes: 8
No: 0

Activity:
• wrote magazine column in support of implants

Activities:
• public rallies
• picketed politicians
• picketed hospitals where implants are performed
• contacted media to request interviews/coverage
• wrote/phoned

18. **Do your family members share your opinion on cochlear implants?**

	ORAL DEAF	SIGNING DEAF
Yes:	8	0
No:	0	7
Not sure:	0	1

19. **Were your parents, siblings, friends, or professional acquaintances (audiologist, speech therapist, etc.) involved in activities related to the cochlear implants controversy? If so, in what way?**

ORAL DEAF		SIGNING DEAF	
Parents	6	Parents	0
Siblings	1	Siblings	1
Friends	3	Friends	8
Prof'l acquaintances	7	Prof'l acquaintances	2**
*Others	6	***Others	4

* Includes professional lobbyists, organizations and professional associations, etc.

** In both cases, these were ASL interpreters.

*** Includes Deaf organizations and two hearing writers sympathetic to Deaf Culture.

Activities:
• personal meetings
• lobbying
• organizational pressure
• writing/phoning
• organized letter-writing campaigns
• "friends in high places"
• media pressure

Activities:
• personal meetings
• writing/phoning
• public rallies

V

REFLECTIONS AND RECOMMENDATIONS

THE FINDINGS OF THIS STUDY are consistent with those of LaMare (1974), Liebschutz and Niemi (1974), and Button (1974), among others, in establishing that a specific marginalized group is socialized early and consistently into political inferiority. The members of the group exhibit alienation, powerlessness, and indifference to the existing dominant system. They either reject it or give it an infantilistic support; do not participate in its conventional political events and institutions; and do not find their interests and concerns reflected in it.

In the case of D/deaf people, these characteristics are the product of a process that began with the selection of a language to be taught to the prelingually deaf child — began, even, with the struggle to obtain a definite diagnosis of deafness. The diagnosis often serves to undermine the parents' confidence in their ability to raise the child and, most important, to make the crucial decisions that will determine the future not only of the child but of the family as a whole.

Oral and Signing D/deaf people alike suffer a "first degree" of marginalization based simply upon the fact that they are deaf and hence stigmatized. Parental responses to this stigma influence the choice of language and identity, which in turn determine the choice of schooling between mainstreaming/integration in hearing schools or segregation in Deaf schools.

ORALISM

Oralism sets integration as its objective, in order that the child may function as an apparent equal within the dominant society. Its fatal flaw is that the deaf child's "biological inheritance", to use Elkin's term, makes successful integration into the mainstream "extremely difficult, if not impossible" (1960:7) and guarantees that the child's equality will only ever be illusory. Such a situation can have a negative impact upon the deaf individual's self-esteem and self-identity, resulting in a passive reliance upon hearing people — particularly parents — to make decisions and to act politically on his/her behalf.

The oralist option is attractive to hearing parents because it stresses the family's role in training the deaf child to "hear" and to speak — a stress that implies the forging of close ties between the family members — and because it proceeds from the reassuring assumption that the child is "normal" and simply needs a little extra attention.

Most parents quite naturally want to keep their child in the family if the alternative is to assign his/her primary socialization to third parties who will introduce him/her to a differing language and culture that the family can never fully share. In this they are encouraged by doctors, audiologists, and others who, by profession, perceive deafness as a deficiency that needs to be "corrected" in order to normalize the child. Normality comes to be defined as speaking and hearing standard language, e.g., English or French. Normalization is expected to lead to successful integration into the social-political system, a goal which in turn implies that successful political socialization will occur by *standard* ("normal") means.

The hearing schools continue and extend oralist methodology by providing a practical training ground for the deaf child to learn how to integrate into the hearing world. Theoretically, the child should be both exhibiting and achieving normality by undergoing the same socialization process that the schools provide for hearing children: that is, taking the same classes as hearing children, socializing with hearing peers, adopting role models from among the hearing school personnel, absorbing hearing values and behaviours, and learning the same political and social information about hearing institutions and systems. But in addition, the deaf child should be practising "hearing" and speaking the same oral-aural language with the same or nearly the same skill and ease as the hearing people surrounding him/her.

There is, however, an inherent contradiction within oralism: its insistence that the child can be normal (i.e., hearing) if his/her deafness is "fixed" serves ironically to focus all attention upon the child's deafness instead of upon his/her normalness. The child, the family, and the professionals alike become dedicated to eradicating the characteristic that stigmatizes the child — an objective which amounts to a denial of the deafness. This denial conflicts with the inescapable physical fact of deafness and can instigate a confusion of identity that leads the child to negative consequences such as passivity, dependence upon others, lack of self-esteem, and a sense of political inefficacy.

The training for integration into the hearing world which is offered through the schools also has problematic results. Peer groups, being composed of hearing persons, confirm the social categorization of the deaf individual as one bearing a stigma; denial or hiding of the stigma by striving to pass as a "fake hearing person" can lead to the discrediting of the individual and a negative perception of his/her deficiency. Even if the deafness is not denied or hidden, the oral deaf child faces an uphill struggle to socialize adequately with hearing peers because of the language and communication barriers that prevent continuously easy interaction. Integration is only apparent: lacking the tools with which to acquire the skills and knowledge of true integration, the child attempts to reflect a competence that he/she neither possesses physically nor feels psychologically.

In the confusion of values and identity that beset the oral deaf individual, reliance upon authority figures such as parents and medical personnel for direction and decision-making persists into adult life. The mature oral deaf person tends to remain a conformist, a passive and dependent person in many important ways, including politically.

MANUALISM

Manualism accepts a large degree of segregation from mainstream society as the price of ensuring that the deaf child may function within the Deaf Culture as a self-actualized person, comfortable within his/her own skin. This is an option that may appeal to those hearing parents who are prepared to accept the differentness of their deaf child, and/or who consider the quick and natural acquisition and mastery of language as most important for the child's development. Its fatal flaw is that it virtually guarantees extreme marginalization; any integration within the dominant society will likely be along the paternalistic lines of the "politics of recognition" as delineated by Taylor (1992), which is to say it is neither true integration nor true equality.

The manualist argument proceeds from the assumption that the prelingually deaf child already is normal, and that his/her normality includes, acknowledges, and accepts (even celebrates) the deafness itself. Manualists insist that deafness is a difference, not a deficiency; the objective should be to manage the difference rather than to attempt an unrealistic obliteration of it.

Management of difference involves recognition of the fact that the deaf child does not hear but can still see, does not speak but can still gesture. A visual-gestural language, Sign language, matches the child's abilities. In order to impart this language to the child, third party socializing agencies are required, because most deaf children are born to hearing parents. The agencies skilled in Sign are part of the Deaf Culture, which has its own values and codes of behaviour. Raising a child within the Deaf Culture creates a unique socializing situation, one in which the family is supplanted as the child's primary socializing agency by a communal presence which will raise him/her within a different language and culture.

One regrettable effect of this situation is that the Signing deaf individual appears to have a more distant relationship with his/her family than the oral deaf person; however, it is clearly possible that this distance is at least as much a result of ongoing communication difficulties between the child and the other family members as it is a result of the transfer of primary socializing responsibility away from the family.

The Deaf schools are acknowledged to be the crucibles of the Deaf Culture, and this burdens them with additional responsibilities for socializing the child. Indeed, they seem presently to be regarded as little *but* training-fields in Deaf Culture, and even that is a job essentially conducted by the student's peer group outside the classroom. As long as the Deaf schools are treated as the "last resort" for educating "oral failures", they have little motivation to improve their academic performances. Dolnick was not being ironic in noting that pedagogy is not the point of these schools (1993:52).

The real irony lies in the fact that the Deaf schools appear to do an excellent job of socializing the deaf child, but it is socialization to an alternate society, not to the dominant one. This is the logical outgrowth of the guiding principle that the deaf child is not deficient but is linguistically and culturally different. Basing his/her schooling upon such a principle naturally stresses the differences and seeks to legitimize them: manual language preferences are acknowledged, Deaf role models (however limited) are provided, the student is segregated socially with his/her Deaf peers, and the latter induct him/her into the Deaf Culture which has its own social and political system.

The mixed messages received by the Deaf student — that it is all right to be a person with deafness, but you cannot expect to accomplish much in the hearing society — appear to result in a more secure self-image, a greater confidence in one's identity, and a strong feeling of community which can lead to political group coherence; but the messages also appear to leave the Deaf naive about hearing society and how it functions. They are, to use the title of Higgins's (1980) book, "outsiders in a hearing world"; a potentially strong political caucus with no penetration into the dominant political structure.

LANGUAGE AS A TOOL OF D/DEAF POLITICAL SOCIALIZATION

The peer group is pivotal in the socialization of the young D/deaf person, particularly with regard to language choice. The oral deaf youth struggles to acquire the hearing peers' oral-aural language through a medium he/she cannot master. Politically, he/she is "colonialized" in Lane's (1992) sense of the term: no matter how skilled he/she may become in the language of the dominant society, he/she will remain forever inferior because he/she can never actually hear the language nor speak it without conscious effort: it remains essentially foreign and acquired (Padden, 1989:10). Even the best of lipreaders cannot accurately catch more than 25 percent of what is spoken. Conrad (1992) found that after ten years of constant training, half of Deaf students actually lipread *worse* than hearing students who had had no training at all. He also reported that despite years of intensive speech therapy, 70 percent of trained Deaf students had indecipherable speech, and only 10 percent had speech good enough to be understood by hearing people. What political efficacy could such people have among a hearing peer group?

Where the language of the peer group is detached from the dominant language of society, as Sign is from the spoken language of any country, the adoption of Sign as one's own language is, willy-nilly, a powerful political statement. It is a form of rejection of the dominant culture, a refusal to be "properly" socialized into that society. Dawson (1977:27-28) calls this a "discontinuity in political socialization"; where the rejection is undertaken deliberately as an act of defiance in the teeth of formal socializing agencies such as the school, it extends discontinuity to the stage of "revolutionary challenge". This is important terminology for understanding recent Deaf political activity. In 1988, eleven years after Dawson's analysis, ASL-fluent Deaf students staged the immensely successful "Deaf President Now" protest at Gallaudet University, and virtually every account of this protest (including contemporaneous mainstream media reports) referred to it as "*the Gallaudet Revolution*". It was indeed a "revolutionary challenge" to the normal system of politically socializing people who are deaf.[1]

---

[1]   See, for example, Gannon (1989), Lane (1992) and Dolnick (1993). Even Kisor (1990), himself an oralist "success", used the term "revolution" in discussing the protest.

Such a "revolutionary challenge" is unthinkable in an oralist context, because oralism aims at minimalizing the discontinuity in political socialization which deafness *qua* deafness threatens to instigate. Becker (1987:63) offers the interesting argument that the Deaf schools and peer groups socialize the child into a variant view of culture, one which sees people as groups; this contrasts to the dominant hearing culture which (at least in Western liberal democracies) sees people generally as individuals. It may be one more reason why the Signing Deaf have been able to cohere as a political force whereas the oral deaf, having been indoctrinated into the hearing culture's individualistic perspective, have lacked comparable impact as a cleavage on the political scene.

POLITICAL SOCIALIZATION AND MARGINALIZATION: A RESPONSE TO TAYLOR

Deaf people appear to be peculiarly caught within the paradox that Taylor (1992) believes arises from confusing "recognition" with "identity". Taylor rejects the argument that marginalization can result from the blow to identity caused by the failure to see oneself reflected in the social mirror, for this is to say that one's identity is shaped by external forces. He holds instead that identity is inwardly generated through an active dialogical process with others, i.e., recognition. This is elegant logic but it presupposes a common language (and a common language mode) through which the dialogue can be successfully conducted. As we have seen, this is exactly what is lacking for the D/deaf individual.

In the case of the Signing person, there is really no language in common with the hearing person even when communication is attempted through the written word, because Sign has no true written form; the Deaf person is forced to function in the hearing person's language (English, for example) and mode (writing), which is an unequal dynamic that can even become oppressive in view of the fact that as many as 65 percent of prelingually Deaf Canadians are functionally illiterate (Carver, 1990). In the case of the oral deaf person, the dialogue may be even more one-sided and oppressive in spite of the fact that both participants are apparently using the same (oral-aural) language, because — as Conrad's (1992) study shows — lipreading and speech training are clearly not equivalent to or substitutable for normal hearing and speech.

This may be taking Taylor's use of the word "dialogue" too literally; the point, however, is that a dialogue by definition cannot take place without mutually coherent communication. Moreover, communication does not consist of language in isolation but arises from and is immersed within specific cultures and values. Taylor raises the question: Whose values? For oral deaf people, the answer is clearly hearing society's values; but those values include and assume hearingness, which is a physical impossibility for a person who is deaf. For Signing people, their culture and values — their very *difference* — are often not accepted by hearing society; it is difficult for hearing people to grasp the concept of a culture that celebrates what the dominant society views as the horrifying calamity of deafness (Dolnick, 1993; Solomon, 1994). To his credit, Taylor recognizes that some cultures are so alien that "we may have only the foggiest idea *ex ante* of in what its valuable contribution might consist. Because, for a sufficiently different culture, the very understanding of what it is to be of worth will be strange and unfamiliar to us" (1992:66-67). In such circumstances, it is inevitable that the alien culture must be marginalized from the larger society.

Taylor's rejection of the "reflection" hypothesis because it concedes too much power to external forces in the shaping of identity likewise seems to take too little account of the special socialization challenges facing D/deaf people. The prelingually D/deaf person's identity is in fact almost *entirely* shaped by external forces during the most important socializing years, beginning with the conscious decision of parents and professionals as to which language will be painstakingly taught to the infant. The relative isolation of D/deaf people, owing to their small numbers and their high likelihood of being born into hearing families, means they will neither see themselves reflected in their primary socializing agencies nor in the larger society; they are consequently more malleable to the external forces because they are unaware of any viable alternative identity. In this they are different from other minorities such as ethnic groups, whose children are born into the same ethnicity as their family members.

For Signing children, reflection is eventually found in the Deaf peer group (an external force), but it is the peer group which also shapes the individual's identity by effectively introducing him/her to the hitherto unexperienced "Deaf" identity. Oral deaf children are even more malleable by external forces: besieged by at least 13 different kinds of "hearing professionals" plus family members from the moment of diagnosis, fitted with technological devices ranging from cochlear implants to hearing aids to tactile aids, immersed in hearing schools and expected to socialize entirely with hearing people, they remain very heavily dependent upon the external forces for their own location and have difficulty in resolving their own identity problems. This is neither recognition *nor* reflection: it is displacement, self-alienation, and marginalization.

REFLECTIONS UPON THE COMPARATIVE GROUP STUDY

The results of the comparative group study appear to support the argument that oralism is a conformist doctrine aimed at inculcating diffuse support for the existing system, whereas manualism embraces segregative choices in order to achieve a comfortable personal identity. The consequences at the family, personal, and social levels, however, remain ambivalent.

Signers may feel secure enough in their identity to insist on using their minority language even where it might impede communication with their loved ones; on the other hand, they may lose or never have the opportunity to develop close family ties, and they may appear selfish and unwilling to deal with the larger society on its own terms. Oral deaf persons may be insecure and lack a clear self-identity, as reflected in their adoption of SimCom, their passive acceptance of their parents' oralist beliefs, and their infantilizing relationship with the latter; but the evidence could just as easily be interpreted to show them as adroit in adapting to their linguistic environment, and as participants in a warm and close family structure.

It appears that both oral and Signing D/deaf people have been socialized to recognize that hearing people control political power, that politics are indeed for "hearies": but whereas oral deaf people aiming at integration do not challenge this message, Signers who have grown up outside the dominant social-political structure believe they can still be efficacious *despite* the hearing nature of politics.

While oral deaf individuals are socialized into political passivity and support for the status quo, the hearing people who are responsible for the precepts and implementation of oralism — parents, schools, the medical profession — are politically astute, influential, and active, both on behalf of the children and in defence of their own efforts to "normalize" them. This is, in effect, a second form or layer of marginalization thrust upon oral deaf people.

Signing individuals seem to defy the received wisdom about standard political socialization, yet develop political interests and act upon them personally. Their second form or layer of marginalization is constructed upon the fact that they remain political outsiders and do not develop strategies that go beyond protest politics; this suggests they are lacking in the political skills, contacts, and knowledge possessed by the hearing members of the "audist establishment".

These conclusions lead to a partial discounting of the theory that Signers are more politically efficacious than the oral deaf merely because of their ability to cohere into a communal force, whereas the oral deaf are individuals absorbed into the greater population. It may be more accurate to say instead that the political potential of the oral deaf is appropriated by their parents and by the "audist" professionals, who are better trained, better able, and better positioned to use the political system for their ends than are the Deaf. It is easier for the oral deaf individual to continue his/her pattern of submission to the authority of hearing people because that is what he/she has been socialized to accept; the Signing community is quicker to act, however unsophisticatedly, on its own behalf, because its members have been socialized to accept themselves as a coherent group of outsiders who have little to risk through "discontinuous" activities.

The ability of the Signers to caucus has enabled them to make gains in fields where benefits to them would also be benefits to others: for example, closed captioning of television programs benefits ten million Canadians of whom only 260,000 are Deaf (the others include the hard of hearing, seniors, children, and language learners); and access to the telephone system via Message Relay Services For the Deaf benefits not just those 260,000 Deaf people but also nearly two million hard of hearing people and the hearing families, friends, and business associates of both Deaf and hard of hearing people (Canadian Association of the Deaf, 1994a,e). Wherever the Deaf have caucused to fight for issues that would directly concern only themselves, however, they have more often met with failure, especially if they faced hearing opposition: cochlear implants are one example, another is the lack of prominence given to Sign as the language of education in most Deaf schools.

Thus, both oral and Signing D/deaf people suffer a "second degree" of marginalization arising directly out of the socialization process. But whereas that of the oral deaf is a marginalization of inculcated passivity, that of the Signing Deaf is one of a lack of access to the political power structure of society.

CONCLUSION

This study has presented arguments and evidence to the effect that conventional political socialization processes are inappropriate for children who are prelingually deaf because such socialization assumes the existence of oral-aural language facility and because it assumes that assimilation into the hearing culture is both suitable and (biologically) possible. D/deaf children do not possess a natural oral-aural facility and may be unable to ever acquire reasonable skills in a "standard" language; and they may prefer assimilation into the Deaf Culture, or be incapable of assimilating into the hearing culture, or may only ever achieve a simulation of integration into it. The result in all cases is a double marginalization.

Further research is needed, particularly empirical data that would extend this paper's study to a wider and more representative sampling. Comparative international data would also be valuable, particularly in the cases of France, where education of the D/deaf is completely oralist and discrimination against them in employment and other fields is legal, and (at the other extreme) in Sweden, where there really are few oral deaf people because of the high social and legal regard for Sign as the language of the D/deaf.

The ultimate objective of such research should be to develop different processes of political socialization for prelingually deaf people which would remove the inevitability of marginalization. Obviously, such ambitions would have to involve major and formidable alterations to several of society's largest and most powerful institutions and agencies. However, the irrefutable proof of the failures of "treatments" and methodologies over the past 115 years, and the apparent success of the contrasting Swedish model (which has a very high rate of professional achievement and literacy among the D/deaf), must be recognized and accepted as ample motivation for the various adherents of both oralist and manualist philosophies to come together to construct a new paradigm shaped upon the strengths and needs of the deaf child, rather than upon the preferences, wishful thinking, and personal stakes of the adults.

More immediate changes would include the following initiatives:

1) conversion of at least one Deaf school in Canada to a full Sign language curriculum and methodology;

2) a fully Deaf administration and faculty in that school;

3) removal of "deafness treatment" (aural rehabilitation, speech therapy, lipreading, and so on) from the regular school-day schedule so that these sessions no longer take away valuable

time from academic subjects; they should be conducted either before or after school-hours, or not at all — after all, what is a school doing providing its students with medical "rehabilitation" instead of education?

4) comprehensive efforts to improve the standards, quality, and results of Deaf education;

5) an end to vocational streaming of D/deaf students;

6) political science courses and political internship programs for D/deaf children and youth;

7) mandatory ASL/LSQ courses in Deaf schools;

8) mandatory ASL/LSQ credit courses for all students (D/deaf and hearing) in hearing schools at which a minimum number of deaf pupils are enrolled, and optional credit courses in schools which have less than this minimum number;

9) the hiring of D/deaf teachers and administrators in both hearing and Deaf schools;

10) specialized training and certification of school interpreters.

Families of deaf children currently receive professional support and advice with regard to educational options, assistive devices, rehabilitation services, and so on; what is lacking is guidance in simply handling the child at home. The families should be provided with attitudinal and behavioural counselling/training through a match-up with D/deaf professionals (not hearing professionals who work with the D/deaf). Such counselling should deal with the area of family politics as well.

These and other alterations to the socializing agencies and processes might affect the "normal" (as distinguished from "normalizing") goals of political socialization. It is intriguing to speculate as to what these altered goals might be. One would hope, however, that they would result in the elimination of automatic double marginalization as a involuntary consequence of deafness.

BIBLIOGRAPHY

Adler, Norman, and Charles Harrington, eds.: *The Learning of Political Behaviour* (Scott, Foresman, Glenview, IL 1970).

Ahlgren, Inger, and Kenneth Hyltenstam, eds.: *Bilingualism in Deaf Education* (Signum, Hamburg, 1994).

Anderson, Glen, and Douglas Watson, eds.: *Innovations in the Habilitation and Rehabilitation of Deaf Adolescents* (University of Arkansas, Little Rock, 1987).

Andersson, Yerker: "International Educational Programs for Deaf Students: Successes and Failures", *AAD Outlook* (Australian Association of the Deaf), Winter 1994.

Anonymous: "Deaf Canadians to march in dozen cities for American Sign Language in schools", *Globe and Mail,* 11 May 1989.

————: "Deaf-learning system slammed", *Halifax Daily News,* 30 January 1989.

Aristotle: *History of Animals* (Penguin Classics, London, 1986).

Atlantic Provinces Special Education Authority (APSEA): *Background Paper for External Analysis of Programs and Services Provided by the Atlantic Provinces Special Education Authority* (APSEA, Halifax, 1994).

Baker, Charlotte, and Robbin Battison, eds.: *Sign Language and the Deaf Community* (National Association of the Deaf, Silver Spring MD, 1980).

Baker, Charlotte, and Dennis Cokely: *American Sign Language: A Teacher's Resource Text on Grammar and Culture* (TJ Publishers, Silver Spring MD, 1980).

Baker-Shenk, Charlotte: "Characteristics of Oppressed and Oppressor Peoples: Their Effect on the Interpreting Context", in McIntire, ed.: *Interpreting the Art of Cross-Cultural Mediation,* 1985.

Barnes, Colin: *Disabled People in Britain and Discrimination* (University of Calgary Press, Calgary, 1991).

Battison, R.: *Lexical Borrowing in American Sign Language* (Linstock Press, Silver Spring MD, 1978).

Baynton, Douglas: "'Savages and Deaf-Mutes': Evolutionary Theory and the Campaign Against Sign Language in the Nineteenth Century", in Van Cleve, ed.: *Deaf History Unveiled*, 1993.

Beam, Dorothy: *The Canadian Association of the Deaf: The First Fifty Years, 1940-1990* (Canadian Association of the Deaf, Toronto-Ottawa, 1990).

Beck, Paul Allen: "The Role of Agents in Political Socialization" in Renshon, ed: *Handbook of Political Socialization*, 1977.

Becker, Gaylene: "Lifelong Socialization and Adaptive Behaviour of Deaf People", in Higgins and Nash, eds.: *Understanding Deafness Socially*, 1987.

Bickenbach, Jerome: *Physical Disability and Social Policy* (University of Toronto Press, Toronto, 1993).

Bissoondath, Neil: "A Question of Belonging: Multiculturalism and Citizenship", in Kaplan, ed.: *Belonging: The Meaning and Future of Canadian Citizenship*, 1993.

Bodner-Johnson, Barbara: "Families That Work for the Hearing-Impaired Child", *The Volta Review*, April 1985.

Bogdan, Robert, and Steven Taylor: "Toward a Sociology of Acceptance: The Other Side of the Study of Deviance", *Social Policy*, Fall 1987.

Brasel, Kenneth, and Stephen Quigley: "Influence of Certain Language and Communication Environments in Early Childhood on the Development of Language in Deaf Individuals", *Journal of Speech and Hearing Research*, 20, 1977.

Brill, Richard: "Interpretation of Least Restrictive Environment", *The Maryland Bulletin*, February-March 1977.

Button, Christine Bennett: "Political Education for Minority Groups", in Niemi, R. and associates, eds.: *The Politics of Future Citizens*, 1974.

Cairns, Alan: *Charter versus Federalism* (McGill-Queen's University Press, Montreal- Kingston, 1992).

————: *Disruptions* (McClelland & Stewart, Toronto, 1991).

Canadian Association of the Deaf (CAD): *Position Paper on Closed Captioning* (Canadian Association of the Deaf, Ottawa, 1994). (a)

————: *Position Paper on Deaf Education* (Canadian Association of the Deaf, Ottawa, 1994). (b)

Canadian Association of the Deaf (CAD): *Position Paper on the Definition of "Deaf"* (Canadian Association of the Deaf, Ottawa, 1994). (c)

————: *Position Paper on Employment and Employability* (Canadian Association of the Deaf, Ottawa, 1994). (d)

————: *Position Paper on Telecommunications* (Canadian Association of the Deaf, Ottawa, 1994). (e)

Carbin, Clifton: *Deaf Heritage in Canada* (McGraw-Hill Ryerson, Toronto, 1996).

Carver, Roger: *A Model Literacy Training Curriculum for the Deaf* (Canadian Association of the Deaf, Ottawa, 1990).

————: *Deaf Illiteracy: A Genuine Educational Puzzle or an Instrument of Oppression?* (Canadian Association of the Deaf, Toronto-Ottawa, 1988). (a)

————: "Least Restrictive Environment: Are They Barking Up the Wrong Tree?", *The Canadian Journal of the Deaf*, vol. 2, no. 1, 1988. (b)

————: "Social Factors in the Development of the Deaf Child", *The Canadian Journal of the Deaf*, vol. 2, no. 2, 1988. (c)

————, and Michael Rodda: "Parental Stress and the Deaf Child", *The ACEHI Journal*, vol. 13, no. 2, 1987.

Carver, Shelly, Elizabeth Doull, Denise Read, Jay Patel, and Valerie Bertin: *Environmental Factors in the Education of Deaf Persons* (Canadian Association of the Deaf, Ottawa, 1991).

Caselli, M. Cristina: "Communication To Language: Deaf Children's and Hearing Children's Development Compared", in McIntire, ed.: *The Acquisition of American Sign Language by Deaf Children*, 1994.

Charrow, Veda, and Ronnie Wilbur: "The Deaf Child as a Linguistic Minority", in Wilcox, ed.: *American Deaf Culture: An Anthology*, 1989.

Clarke, Harold, Jane Jenson, Lawrence Le Duc, and Jon Pammett: *Absent Mandate* (Gage, Toronto, 1991).

Cohen, O.: "An Integrated Summer Recreation Program", *The Volta Review*, no. 73, 1969.

Conrad, Reuben: "Towards a Definition of Oral Success", in Lee, ed.: *Deaf Liberation*, 1992.

Davis, Fred: "Deviance and Disavowal: The Management of Strained Interaction by the Visibly Handicapped", *Social Problems*, no. 9, 1961.

Dawson, Richard, and Kenneth Prewitt: *Political Socialization*, 1st ed. (Little, Brown, Toronto, 1969).

————, and Karen Dawson: *Political Socialization*, 2nd ed. (Little, Brown, Toronto, 1977).

Dean, Mary, and Jennifer Nettles: "Reverse Mainstreaming: A Successful Model for Interaction", *The Volta Review*, vol. 89, no. 1, January 1987.

Desselle, Debra: "Self-Esteem, Family Climate, and Communication Patterns in Relation to Deafness", *American Annals of the Deaf*, vol. 139, no. 3, July 1994.

Di Carlo, Louis: *The Deaf* (Prentice-Hall, Englewood Cliffs NJ, 1964).

Doe, Tanis: *Ontario Schooling and the Status of the Deaf: An Enquiry into Inequality, Status Assignment, and Educational Power* (unpublished MSW thesis, Carleton University, 1988).

————: "The Social Construction of Deaf Women", *Women's Education des femmes*, vol. 12, no. 2, Summer 1996.

Dolnick, Edward: "Deafness As Culture", *The Atlantic*, vol. 272, no. 3, September 1993.

Draper, Roger: "A Voice of Silence", *The New Leader*, 29 June 1992.

Driedger, Diane: *The Last Civil Rights Movement* (Hurst, London, 1989).

Easton, David, and Jack Dennis: *Children in the Political System* (McGraw-Hill, New York, 1969).

Eisenstadt, S.N.: "Archetypal Patterns of Youth", *Daedalus*, Winter, 1962.

Elkin, Frederick: *The Child and Society: The Process of Socialization* (Random House, New York, 1960).

Elshtain, Jean Bethke: *Democracy On Trial* (Anansi, Concord, 1993).

Emerson, Richard: "Power-Dependency Relations", *American Sociological Review*, no. 27, 1962.

Erting, Carol: *Deafness, Communication, Social Identity: Ethnography in a Preschool for Deaf Children* (Linstok Press, Burtonsville MD, 1994).

Etzioni, Amitai: *The Active Society* (Free Press, New York, 1968).

Fine, Michelle, and Adrienne Asch: "Disability Beyond Stigma: Social Interaction, Discrimination, and Activism", in Nagler, ed.: *Perspectives on Disability*, 1990.

Fischer, Renate, and Harlan Lane, eds.: *Looking Back* (Signum, Hamburg, 1993).

Freire, Paulo: *Pedagogy of the Oppressed* (Continuum, New York, 1970).

Friedenberg, E.Z., ed.: *The Anti-American Generation* (Transaction, New Jersey, 1971).

Friedman, L.A.: "The Manifestation of Subject, Object, and Topic in American Sign Language", in Li, ed.: *Subject and Topic*, 1976.

Gannon, Jack: *Deaf Heritage* (National Association of the Deaf, Silver Spring, 1981).

———: *The Week the World Heard Gallaudet* (Gallaudet University Press, Washington DC, 1989).

Gee, James Paul, and Wendy Goodhart: "Nativization, Linguistic Theory, and Deaf Language Acquisition" in McIntire, ed.: *The Acquisition of American Sign Language by Deaf Children*, 1994.

Gentile, Augustus, and Sal DiFrancesca: *Academic Achievement Test Performance of Hearing Impaired Students in the United States*. Series D, no. 1, Gallaudet College Office of Demographic Studies (Gallaudet College, Washington DC, 1969).

Gergen, Kenneth, and Matthew Ullman: "Socialization and the Characterological Basis of Political Activism", in Renshon, ed.: *Handbook of Political Socialization*, 1977.

Glickman, N.: "The War of the Languages", *The Deaf American*, vol. 36, no. 6, 1984.

Goffman, Erving: *Stigma* (Touchstone, New York, 1963).

Goldfarb, Martin, and Thomas Axworthy: *Marching to a Different Drummer* (Stoddart, Toronto, 1988).

Greenstein, Fred: *Children and Politics*, rev. ed. (Yale University Press, New Haven, 1965).

———: "Political Socialization", in Sills, D.L., ed.: *International Encyclopaedia of the Social Sciences* (Macmillan, New York, 1968).

Groce, Nora Ellen: *Everyone Here Spoke Sign Language* (Harvard University Press, Cambridge, 1985).

Hahn, Harlan: "The Politics of Physical Differences: Disability and Discrimination", *Journal of Social Issues*, vol. 44, no. 1, 1988.

Hallowell, Davis, and S. Richard Silverman: *Hearing and Deafness* (Holt, Rinehart and Winston, New York, 1970).

Heller, K., ed.: *Psychosocial Interventions with Sensorially Disabled Persons* (Grune and Stratton, New York, 1986).

Hess, Robert, and Judith Torney: *The Development of Political Attitudes in Children* (Aldine, Chicago, 1967).

Higgins, Paul: *Outsiders in a Hearing World* (Sage, Beverley Hills, 1980).

————, and Jeffrey Nash, eds.: *Understanding Deafness Socially* (Charles Thomas, Springfield MA, 1987).

Hyman, Herbert: *Political Socialization* (Free Press, New York, 1959).

Israelite, Nita: "On Readability Forumulas: A Critical Analysis for Teachers of the Deaf", *American Annals of the Deaf,* no. 123, 1988.

Ivers, Kathryn: "Towards a Bilingual Education Policy in the Mainstreaming of Deaf Children", *Columbia Human Rights Law Review,* vol. 26, no. 439, 1995.

Jacobs, Leo: *A Deaf Adult Speaks Out,* 3rd ed. (Gallaudet University Press, Washington DC, 1989).

Kannapell, Barbara: *Language Choice - Identity Choice* (Linstok Press, Burtonsville MD, 1993).

————: "Personal Awareness and Advocacy in the Deaf Community", in Baker and Battison, eds.: *Sign Language and the Deaf Community,* 1980.

Kaplan, William, ed.: *Belonging: The Meaning and Future of Canadian Citizenship* (McGill-Queen's University Press, Montreal-Kingston, 1993).

Kisor, Henry: *What's That Pig Outdoors* (Hill and Wang, New York, 1990).

Klima, Edward, and Ursula Bellugi: *The Signs of Language* (Harvard University Press, Cambridge, 1979).

Kluwin, Thomas, and Martha Gonter Gaustad: "The Role of Adaptability and Communication in Fostering Cohesion in Families with Deaf Adolescents", *American Annals of the Deaf,* vol. 139, no. 3, July 1994.

Knutson, J.N., ed.: *Handbook of Political Psychology* (Jossey-Bass, San Francisco, 1973).

Krause, Elliot: "Structured Strain in a Marginal Profession: Rehabilitation Counselling", *Journal of Health and Social Behaviour,* vol. 6, 1965.

Kyle, J.G., and B. Woll: *Sign Language: The Study of Deaf People and Their Language* (Cambridge University Press, Cambridge, 1985).

Kymlicka, Will: *Recent Work in Citizenship Theory* (Multiculturalism and Citizenship Canada, Ottawa, 1992).

Ladd, Paddy: "1st Epistle to the Teacher of the Deaf", in Lee, ed.: *Deaf Liberation,* 1992.(a)

————: "3rd Epistle to the Teacher of the Deaf", in Lee, ed.: *Deaf Liberation,* 1992.(b)

LaMare, James: "Language Environment and Political Socialization of Mexican-American Children", in Niemi and associates, eds.: *The Politics of Future Citizens*, 1974.

Lamont, Mary: "Where Have All the Provincial Schools Gone?" *ACEHI Educator*, Association of Canadian Educators of the Hearing Impaired, vol. 17, no. 2, March 1994.

Lane, Harlan: *When the Mind Hears* (Random House, New York, 1984).

————: *The Mask of Benevolence* (Knopf, New York, 1992).

Langton, Kenneth: "Peer Group and School and the Political Socialization Process", in Adler and Harrington, eds.: *The Learning of Political Behaviour*, 1970.

Lee, Raymond, ed.: *Deaf Liberation* (National Union of the Deaf, Middlesex, 1992).

Levitt, E., and S. Cohen: "Attitudes of Children Toward Their Handicapped Peers", *Childhood Education*, 52, 1976.

Li, C.N., ed.: *Subject and Topic* (Academic Press, New York, 1976).

Liebschutz, Sarah, and Richard Niemi: "Political Attitudes among Black Children", in Niemi and associates, eds.: *The Politics of Future Citizens*, 1974.

Loeb, Roger, and Pamela Sarigiani: "The Impact of Hearing Impairment on Self-Perceptions of Children", *The Volta Review*, vol. 88, no. 2, February/March 1986.

Marcuse, Herbert: *One-Dimensional Man* (Beacon Press, Boston, 1964).

Markowicz, Harry: "Some Sociolinguistic Considerations of American Sign Language", in Stokoe, ed.: *Sign and Culture*, 1980.

Marshall, T.H.: *Class, Citizenship, and Social Development* (Anchor Books, Garden City NY, 1965).

———— , and Tom Bottomore: *Citizenship and Social Class* (Pluto Press, London, 1992).

Mason, David: *Bilingual/Bicultural Deaf Education is Appropriate.* Occasional Monograph Series, no. 2, Association of Canadian Educators of the Hearing Impaired, 1994.

————: *Mainstream Education and Deaf Students* (Canadian Association of the Deaf, Ottawa, 1996).

McCartney, Brian David: "An Investigation of the Factors Contributing to the Ability of Hearing-Impaired Children to Communicate Orally as Perceived by Oral Deaf Adults and

Parents and Teachers of the Hearing Impaired", *The Volta Review*, vol. 88, no. 3, April 1986.

McIntire, Marina, ed.: *The Acquisition of American Sign Language by Deaf Children* (Linstok Press, Burtonsville MD, 1994).

———: *Interpreting the Art of Cross-Cultural Mediation: Proceedings of the 1985 Registry of Interpreters of the Deaf Convention* (RID, 1985).

McRoberts, Kenneth, and Patrick Monahan: *The Charlottetown Accord, the Referendum, and the Future of Canada* (University of Toronto Press, Toronto, 1993).

Meadow, Kathryn: "Early Manual Communication in Relation to the Deaf Child's Intellectual, Social, and Communicative Functioning", *American Annals of the Deaf*, no. 113, 1968.

Meadow-Orlans, Kathryn: "Understanding Deafness: Socialization of Children and Youth", in Higgins and Nash, eds.: *Understanding Deafness Socially*, 1987.

Merker, Hannah: *Listening* (HarperPerennial, New York, 1992).

Nagler, Mark, ed.: *Perspectives on Disability* (Health Markets Research, Palo Alto CA, 1990).

Nash, Jeffrey, and Anedith Nash: *Deafness In Society* (Heath, Lexington MA, 1981).

———: "Deafness and Family Life in Modern Society", in Higgins and Nash, eds.: *Understanding Deafness Socially*, 1987.

Niemi, Richard, and associates, eds.: *The Politics of Future Citizens* (Jossey-Bass, San Francisco, 1974).

Notoya, Masako, Shigetada Suzuki, and Mitsuru Furukawa: "Effects of Early Manual Instruction on the Oral-Language Development of Two Deaf Children", *American Annals of the Deaf*, vol. 139, no. 3, July 1994.

Padden, Carol: "The Deaf Community and the Culture of Deaf People", in Wilcox, ed.: *American Deaf Culture*, 1989.

———, and Tom Humphries: *Deaf in America: Voices From a Culture* (Harvard University Press, Cambridge, 1988).

Parasnis, Ila, ed.: *Cultural and Language Diversity and the Deaf Experience* (Cambridge University Press, Cambridge, 1996).

Patterson, Franklin: "Political Reality in Childhood: Dimensions of Education for Citizenship", reprinted in Adler and Harrington, eds.: *The Learning of Political Behaviour*, 1963.

Petitto, Laura Ann: "Are Signed Languages 'Real' Languages? Evidence from American Sign Language and Langue des Signes Quebecoise", *Signpost*, vol. 7, no. 3, Autumn 1994.

Petitto, Laura Ann, and Paula Marentette: "Babbling in the Manual
    Mode: Evidence for the Ontogeny of Language", *Science*,
    vol. 251, no. 22, March 1991.
Pinker, Steven: *The Language Instinct: How the Mind Creates
    Language* (William Morrow, New York, 1994).
Powell, Frank, Terese Finitzo-Hieber, Sandy Friel-Patti, and Donald
    Henderson, eds.: *Education of the Hearing Impaired Child*
    (College-Hill Press, San Diego, 1985).
Reich, Carol, D. Hambelton, and B. Houdin: "The Integration of
    Hearing Impaired Children in Regular Classrooms", *American
    Annals of the Deaf*, no. 122, 1977.
Renshon, Stanley Allen, ed.: *Handbook of Political Socialization* (Free
    Press, New York, 1977).
Roots, James: PAH!-*litics: Deaf and Disabled Political Participation and
    Activity* (Canadian Association of the Deaf, Ottawa, 1992).
Rose, Arnold: "Incomplete Socialization", *Sociology and Social
    Relations*, vol. 44, 1960.
Rosenberg, Morris: "Self-Esteem and Concern with Public Affairs",
    Public Opinion Quarterly, vol. 26, no. 2, Summer 1962.
Rutherford, Susan: *A Study of American Deaf Folklore* (Linstok Press,
    Burtonsville MD, 1993).
Sacks, Oliver: *Seeing Voices* (University of California Press,
    Berkeley/Los Angeles, 1989).
Schein, Jerome: *At Home Among Strangers* (Gallaudet University
    Press, Washington DC, 1989).
————: *Canadians with Impaired Hearing.* Statistics Canada Post-
    Censal Surveys Program, Special Topic Series from the Health
    and Activities Limitation Survey. (Minister of Industry, Science
    and Technology, Ottawa, 1992.)
————: *The Deaf Community: Studies in the Social Psychology of
    Deafness* (Gallaudet University Press, Washington DC, 1968).
———— , and Marcus Delk: *The Deaf Population of the United States*
    (National Association of the Deaf, Silver Spring MD, 1974).
Schlesinger, Hilde: "Deafness, Mental Health, and Language", in
    Powell *et al.*, eds.: *Education of the Hearing Impaired Child*, 1985.
————: "Dialogue in Many Worlds: Adolescents and Adults -
    Hearing and Deaf", in Anderson, Glen, and Douglas Watson,
    eds.: *Innovations in the Habilitation and Rehabilitation of Deaf
    Adolescents*, 1987.

Schlesinger, Hilde: "Effects of Powerlessness on Dialogue and Development: Disability, Poverty, and the Human Condition", in Heller, ed.: *Psychosocial Interventions with Sensorially Disabled Persons*, 1986.

Schwartz, Howard: "Further Thoughts on a 'Sociology of Acceptance' for Disabled People", *Journal of Social Policy*, Fall 1988.

Seeman, Melvin: "Alienation Studies", *Annual Review of Sociology*, vol. 1, 1975.

————: "On the Meaning of Alienation", *American Sociological Review*, vol. 24, no. 6, December 1959.

Sigel, Roberta: *Learning About Politics* (Random House, New York, 1970).

Sigurdson, Richard: "Preston Manning and the Politics of Postmodernism in Canada", *Canadian Journal of Political Science*, vol. 27, no. 2, June 1994.

Silverman, S. Richard: "From Aristotle to Bell - and Beyond" in Hallowell and Silverman: *Hearing and Deafness*, 1970.

Snider, Bruce, ed.: *Inclusion? Defining Quality Education for Deaf and Hard of Hearing Students* (Gallaudet University, Washington DC, 1995).

Solomon, Andrew: "Defiantly Deaf", *New York Times Magazine*, 28 August 1994.

Sourds en colère: "Demo Against Cochlear Implant", international report distributed to national Deaf associations including the Canadian Association of the Deaf (Lyon, France, 1993).

Spicer, Keith: *Citizens' Forum on Canada's Future* (Supply and Services Canada, Ottawa, 1991).

"Starr, Carrie Davis" (pseud.): "Deaf Students in the Mainstream: A School Counsellor's Journal", *Deaf Life*, vol. 7, no. 3, September 1994.

Stein, Laszlo, Eugene Mindel, and Theresa Jabaley: *Deafness and Mental Health* (Grune and Stratton, New York, 1981).

Stevens, Raymond: "Children's Language Should Be Learned and Not Taught", in Stokoe, ed.: *Sign and Culture*, 1980.

Stinson, Michael, and Irene Leigh: "Inclusion and the Psycho-social Development of Deaf Children and Youths", in Snider, ed.: *Inclusion? Defining Quality of Education for Deaf and Hard of Hearing Students*, 1995.

Stokoe, William, Dorothy Casterline, and Carl Croneberg: *A Dictionary of American Sign Language on Linguistic Principles* (TJ Publishers, Silver Spring MD, 1965).

Stokoe, William, ed.: "Dimensions of Difference: ASL and English-Based Cultures", in Wilcox, ed.: *American Deaf Culture*, 1989.

————: *Sign and Culture* (Linstok Press, Silver Spring MD, 1980).

————: *Sign Language Structure* (Linstok Press, Burtonsville MD, 1960).

———— , and Battison, Robbin: "Sign Language, Mental Health, and Satisfactory Interaction", in Stein *et al.*, eds.: *Deafness and Mental Health*, 1981.

Stuckless, Ross, and Jack Birch: "The Influence of Early Manual Communication on the Linguistic Development of Deaf Children", *American Annals of the Deaf*, no. 111, 1966.

Sussman, Marvin: "A Policy Perspective on the United States Rehabilitation System", *Journal of Health and Social Behaviour*, vol. 13, 1972.

Taylor, Charles: *Multiculturalism and "The Politics of Recognition"* (Princeton University Press, Princeton, 1992).

Valli, Clayton, Ceil Lucas; Esmé Farb, and Paul Hulick, eds.: *ASL Pah! Deaf Students' Perspectives on Their Language* (Linstok Press, Burtonsville MD, 1992). Also an accompanying videotape of the same name.

Van Cleve, John, ed.: *Deaf History Unveiled* (Gallaudet University Press, Washington DC, 1993).

————: "The Academic Integration of Deaf Children: A Historical Perspective", in Fischer and Lane, eds.: *Looking Back*, 1993.

Vector Public Opinion Report, Marc Zwelling, ed.: January, February, April, and May 1993 issues.

Vernon, McCay, and Charles C. Estes: "Deaf Leadership and Political Activism", in *The Deaf American*, November 1975.

Vernon, McCay, and S.D. Koh: "Early Manual Communication and Deaf Children's Achievement", *American Annals of the Deaf*, no. 115, 1970.

Vlug, Henry: *ASL/LSQ Laws and Deaf Laws* (Canadian Association of the Deaf, Ottawa, 1995).

Warren, Charlotte, and Suzanne Hasenstab: "Self-Concept of Severely to Profoundly Hearing-Impaired Children", *The Volta Review*, vol. 88, no. 6, October/November 1986.

Weinstein, G.: "Nursery School with a Difference", *Parents*, vol. 11, no. 43, 1968.

Whitaker, Reg: *A Sovereign Idea* (McGill-Queen's University Press, Montreal-Kingston, 1992).

White, Elliott: "Intelligence and Sense of Political Efficacy in Children", *Journal of Politics*, vol. 30, no. 3, August 1968.

Wilcox, Sherman, ed.: *American Deaf Culture: An Anthology* (Linstok Press, Burtonsville MD, 1989).

Woodward, James: "How You Gonna Get To Heaven If You Can't Talk with Jesus?: The Educational Establishment vs. the Deaf Community", in Wilcox, ed.: *American Deaf Culture: An Anthology*, 1989.

———, and Harry Markowicz: "Pidgin Sign Languages", in Stokoe, ed.: *Sign and Culture*, 1985.

Woolley, Maggie: "Signs of Strife - Signs of Life", in Lee, ed.: *Deaf Liberation*, 1992.

World Federation of the Deaf: *Proceedings of the 1991 World Congress of the Deaf* (World Federation of the Deaf, Helsinki, 1991).

Wright, David: *Deafness* (Faber and Faber, London, 1969).

Yinger, J.M.: "Anomie, Alienation, and Political Behaviour", in Knutson, ed.: *Handbook of Political Psychology*, 1973.

Young, Iris Marion: *Justice and the Politics of Difference* (Princeton University Press, Princeton, 1990).

Zureik, Elia, and Robert Pike, eds.: *Socialization and Values in Canadian Society, vol. 1: Political Socialization* (Carleton Library Series/Macmillan, Ottawa, 1978).

Zweibel, Abraham, Kathryn Meadow-Orlans, and Birgit Dyssegaard: "A Comparison of Hearing Impaired Students in Israel, Denmark, and the United States", *International Journal of Rehabilitation Research*, 9, 1986.